My Return to Love

A Journey from the Depths of Brokenness to the Heights of Self Love

Helen Taylor

First published by Ultimate World Publishing 2023
Copyright © 2023 Helen Taylor

ISBN

Paperback: 978-1-923123-36-6
Ebook: 978-1-923123-37-3

Helen Taylor has asserted her rights under the Copyright, Designs and Patents Act 1988 to be identified as the author of this work. The information in this book is based on the author's experiences and opinions. The publisher specifically disclaims responsibility for any adverse consequences which may result from use of the information contained herein. Permission to use information has been sought by the author. Any breaches will be rectified in further editions of the book.

All rights reserved. No part of this publication may be reproduced, stored in or introduced into a retrieval system, or transmitted in any form, or by any means (electronic, mechanical, photocopying, recording or otherwise) without the prior written permission of the author. Any person who does any unauthorised act in relation to this publication may be liable to criminal prosecution and civil claims for damages. Enquiries should be made through the publisher.

Cover design: Ultimate World Publishing
Layout and typesetting: Ultimate World Publishing
Editor: Alex Floyd-Douglass

Ultimate World Publishing
Diamond Creek,
Victoria Australia 3089
www.writeabook.com.au

DISCLAIMER

This book is a memoir and a guide for transformation.

It reflects the author's present recollections of experiences over time, and can only be told with the truth and nothing but the truth.

The events and conversations in this book have been set down to the best of the author's ability. No harm or disrespect is intended.

DEDICATION

To my sons.

You were my purpose and I am forever grateful.

To my mum.

Thank you for always listening. I finally figured it all out!

CONTENTS

Disclaimer	iii
Dedication	v
The Voice Told Me To 'Get Out'	ix
Introduction	1
Chapter 1: What Is This Place: Heaven Or Hell?	3
Chapter 2: The Relationships That Shaped Me	21
Chapter 3: The Potential	33
Chapter 4: I Think I Met My Dad	45
Chapter 5: I Think I Met Myself	63
Chapter 6: The Game Changer	79
Chapter 7: Past Lives, Spirit Guides And Demons	103
Chapter 8: Karma, Life And Death	119
Chapter 9: I 'Knew' It Was Time To Swap Roles	137
Chapter 10: Will This Ride Ever Stop?	157
Chapter 11: Revelations	165
Afterword	171
About The Author	175
Adamantine Healing Australia	177

THE VOICE TOLD ME TO 'GET OUT'

This seems like a really good place to start because this one event was really important and was going to change my life forever.

Let me set the scene for you… I'm 33 years old and have been married for seven years. I have three beautiful boys, Cameron, who is six years old and twins, Shane and Gavin, who are both four years old. My husband David is at work and the kids are at school and kindergarten respectively.

I am at home alone getting the housework done. I'm standing at the kitchen sink mindlessly doing the dishes and gazing out the window over the backyard.

A voice from somewhere behind me and a few feet above my right shoulder declared, *"Get out."*

My Return To Love

I can be very specific because I've analysed this moment over and over again. It's a loud, clear voice and instantly, I freeze.

In that instant, I had so much information downloaded all at once.

I know the voice is right. It knows my marriage is over, it knows I've tried many ways to save it but none of them have worked, it knows there is nothing else I can do, it knows it's time for me to get out and it knows I'm terrified at that thought.

It knows all my thoughts.

I have three kids: how will I survive? How will I have money? How will I feed them?

All these thoughts are flooding through my mind together with tons of images flooding my mind all at once.

What the hell was happening to me?

Mentally I do the check – husband at work, kids at school and kindergarten, no one is home…

I am alone.

So, who the hell just spoke to me?

I didn't consider myself a religious person at all, so God never crossed my mind. But I did have to look; I had to check to make sure that no one really was there.

I slowly turned around and… No one was there.

The Voice Told Me To 'Get Out'

I just couldn't process it, so I went back to doing the dishes, but it happened again. This time the voice boomed, *"Get out now!"*

It was incredible, this voice was telling me exactly what I already knew, that the marriage was over, and I had to leave.

It seemed to support me somehow – while giving me clear directions. I also realised something else that was conveyed to me at the same time, it was a 'knowing' and you just can't explain knowing.

The knowing was that if I stayed married to David, I was going to die.

INTRODUCTION

This book is for everyone who has ever felt lost, alone and broken.

I know you very well and I figured it all out.

I extend my hand to you – not as someone who has all the answers, but as a guide who has navigated the depths of my soul and emerged stronger and wiser on the other side.

I share my story not for sympathy, but because I believe now in my power and the power of something even greater that I discovered along the way.

I wrote these words not merely to inspire you, but to encourage change.

I want you to know that the shackles that bind you can be broken, the cycles that confine you can be shattered and the love that seems so distant can be found within your own heart.

My Return To Love

I also know that, just by reading this book, you will change for the better, you will begin to transform and slowly rise above whatever – or whoever – it is that has been holding you back.

Because you, my friend, are not merely a collection of broken pieces; you are a grand masterpiece. The greatest creation on this earth.

You are love.

This is not just my book; it is my lifeline. I offer it to you with the hope that it becomes a source of strength to you and a reminder that, no matter how deep the abyss, there is always a way out.

Let us begin this journey together.

Chapter 1

WHAT IS THIS PLACE: HEAVEN OR HELL?

Before I go into my childhood, I would like to declare something.

There is a little girl inside of me. She was severely abused and traumatised during the first 10 years of her life. So, I am going to begin first by taking hold of her and taking care of her before I begin to tell our story.

This isn't very easy for either of us.

I want to thank her for her bravery and for letting me tell her story because, without it, what happened to me later in life wouldn't have made as much sense to you at all.

On 15th April 1961, I was born into this world; so innocent and so pure. I had blonde hair that was almost white and big, blue eyes.

I was filled with so much love.

Unfortunately, love wasn't valued highly in the family I was born into. My dad didn't have love; he was broken. My mum had an enormous heart, but she wasn't allowed to use it much.

You'll find out why as we continue this journey.

MUM AND DAD

Let me explain a little about Mum and Dad.

Mum was a natural beauty with a big, beautiful heart and so full of wonder. Her name was Dorothy.

> *INSIGHT: What I mean by wonder is innocence. This is something really important to understand. Some people call it being naive but it's actually a beautiful innocence that really does see the world as a place full of wonder. I know that feeling because I have lived my life that way, too.*

She was one of four children – an older and younger sister and a younger brother – born to hard-working parents who were pillars of the Deniliquin community. Her mother ran the home like clockwork; her father was a tough man, no-nonsense.

She followed her oldest sister to the city. She was a country girl who left home to go to the 'big smoke' and follow her dreams. She found herself a job and enjoyed two of her loves, playing tennis and travelling. It wasn't long before she had saved up and bought herself a *Morris Minor*. A very nice car for the times.

Dad was an only child, raised in the inner suburbs of Melbourne; his name was Ronald. He has a very different story to Mum.

His father was Albert; Dad was the product of Albert's second marriage. Albert had a daughter from the first marriage, Winifred, who had been one of twins. The twin and Albert's first wife both died in childbirth. Dad's mother, Jean, was the second wife.

Dad lost his left arm from gangrene at the age of eight; it was amputated just below the shoulder. Not long after that, he lost his father.

His mother really didn't like children. After Albert's death, she sent the stepsister, Winifred, away to live with her maternal grandmother.

Dad suffered a lot of trauma at such a young age and, unfortunately, that shaped his view of the world.

> *INSIGHT: Later in my life I would learn more about my dad's mother during conversations with his stepsister, my Auntie Win. Dad's mum was not a very nice person. She was very self-absorbed and not very maternal. Unfortunately, our parents teach us how to be parents – the good and the bad.*

Dad was a handsome man who loved football and cricket. He was driven; he was going to make something of himself no matter what.

Mum and Dad met at the Hawthorn Town Hall; regular dances were held there and were a great way to meet other people and have some fun. After a whirlwind romance, they were married on the 2nd July 1960, then quickly got pregnant and along came me.

Something was wrong though, because I don't think Dad wanted kids. He certainly didn't want me around and that became apparent very, very quickly.

The stories I am about to share were talked about many times throughout my life, but I can't actually remember them myself. Isn't it funny that you can't remember a lot of your childhood, but some significant events just stand out?

The following are two events I can still recall.

PARENTING PATTERNS REPEAT

At around 18 months old, my dad drove me to my Auntie Win's and tried to leave me there. Auntie Win refused and sent him back home. He got really angry.

On the way home, he slammed on the brakes of the car while I was standing next to him on the bench seat (yes, this was before seatbelts), and I smacked my face into the dashboard of the car.

I remember the horrified look on Mum's face when she walked out the front door of the house to greet us and saw me covered in blood and missing a few baby teeth.

He told her it was an accident. I remember them arguing. They argued a lot.

This was just the beginning of the many things he did to me.

He terrified me. He was nasty. He was a quiet threat.

From the ages of four to 10, my father abused me. He came into my room at night, molested me and poisoned my mind with his words. He warned me of many things; he said I would die if I told anyone, I had to hold the blankets up over my head and not make any noise or someone would come and cut off my ears.

> *INSIGHT: You know I slept with the doona over my ears right up until I was in my 30s and never questioned why! I only stopped because one day, I wondered why I was even doing it.*

There were times he would nearly get caught but he pretended to be playing games with me, being a ghost and shaking my bed or hiding under my bed.

Hiding under my bed became another weird trigger in later life.

From time to time, I would have a problem sitting up in bed and hanging my feet over the side. I would have an unrealistic thought of someone grabbing my ankles. And, of course, I was afraid of the dark.

The things he did to me systematically broke me down and convinced me that I was a mistake, that I should have never been born and that I was useless.

Worthless.

Memories of these times were never far from my mind. The memories came back to me strongly years later in my late 30's, as old dreams began to resurface.

All throughout my childhood, I had recurring dreams. There was a big dog that would grab me as I was coming home from school. The dog would either drop me down the drain down the street from our house or take me to a park where there was a large home surrounded by a high wire fence and it would throw me over the fence into the home. It wasn't a nice home to visit.

These weren't dreams; they were nightmares.

I would also have recurring thoughts while I was awake at night. Thoughts and visions of being stabbed. They were the strangest things to think of and experience. I wasn't really being stabbed but why was I so worried about it?

I had no clue.

Dad went to great lengths to make sure I would say nothing. Whenever no one else was around or no one else was home, he would tell me repeatedly how worthless I was, how useless I was.

I remember being seven years old and he was so angry; he was in a rage. His face was white, and spit was coming from his mouth. He was inches from my face and quietly poisoning my mind. I challenged him to hit me because I knew he really wanted to. He flew off in a rage.

Lucky for me, I think, because he had the potential to beat me up, but he never did physically.

One of the things I really struggled to understand was when he would come back to me later after times of abusing me and say, *"But you know I love though, you know that, don't you?"*

This would leave me so confused. His behaviour said he hated me, but he loved me?

All it would take was to hear his car come down the driveway at night and my heart would sink and the anxiety would rise.

I never knew what mood would walk in the door. I learned how to adapt my behaviour to whatever mood he was in. Always trying to be a good girl; learning how to be a 'good girl' to make everyone else happy.

This was the beginning of the bed wetting.

THE TRAUMA OF BED WETTING

Bed wetting coincided with urinary tract infections (UTIs). Mum said I would get them over and over again between the ages of four and 10. Mum did the usual thing and took me to the doctor.

She was bewildered because she would say that every time she took me to the doctor, the infection would stop. They got the bed-wetting mattress, one with a bell. As soon as the mattress got wet, the bell would go off.

How embarrassing, how humiliating. I hated it; it did nothing. But it did stop Dad's visits.

Nothing stopped the bed wetting and now it was becoming a bigger problem because I was even having problems actually 'holding on' during the day. There were a number of times at school when I wet my pants – when I wasn't quick enough to get to the toilet or when the teachers wouldn't let me leave the classroom.

There were also times when I just didn't make it home in time; it was embarrassing and humiliating.

Back to the doctor I went and then, to the specialist for some awful and embarrassing procedures and x-rays, then finally, to the surgeon. I went through so much and, at the age of 10, in September of 1971, I went to hospital and had a major operation.

The bilateral re-implantation of ureters.

You see both urethras were broken away from my bladder. This meant that when I got a signal to pee; I had to immediately. There was no way to 'hold on'.

The doctor couldn't say how it happened. He said I could have been born that way, or it happened as I grew.

I remember being in the hospital.

It was St Georges in Kew which, at the time, was not a hospital for children. I was an exception. I remember going into surgery. The surgeon asked me if I had any questions; I did.

Could he show me the knife he was going to use? He agreed and asked me to start counting back from 10. I never did get to see the knife.

I remember waking up in the hospital bed after the surgery. I was in a ward right at the end of the corridor.

Down the corridor, I could see the nurses' station. As I came around from the anaesthetic, I started to feel awful, like I was going to vomit, so I used the buzzer.

What Is This Place: Heaven Or Hell?

I could see the nurses; they were talking to each other but no one was noticing my buzzer. I started to panic; I was going to throw up and I had to get their attention.

That's when this lady appeared next to my bed. I hadn't noticed her until now. She never said a word to me, she just made me feel calm.

The nurses arrived and I never gave that lady another thought.

Now, let's fast forward to 25 years later.

I'm sat at the kitchen table with Mum and we're going through lots of old photos. I came across a photo of a woman with a young boy and I asked Mum who it was, "Oh, that's your dad and his mother Jean," she replied.

I was stunned, this was the woman who visited me in the hospital.

I told Mum that I had met her, that she was the woman next to my bed when I was in hospital. *"It couldn't have been her,"* Mum declared. *"She died before you were born."*

I had never seen a picture of my dad's mother until then. It was definitely her; she was the woman from the hospital.

In total, I was in hospital for a few weeks, with many more weeks at home recovering.

THE OBEDIENT, COMPLIANT CHILD IS COMPLETE

Can you see the full picture yet? Let me set it out…

By the time I was 10 years old, I was convinced that I was useless and worthless; I was a mistake and didn't deserve to be here. In fact, everything that went wrong WAS my fault. That same thinking was now going to form my behaviour and the future events in my life.

Don't get me wrong – not all of my childhood was bad. Dad was rising up through the ranks with Alcoa. He was a salesman and a very good one. Mum enjoyed raising us kids and running the household. She loved her weekly games of tennis and took us to church every Sunday.

Dad wasn't very kind to her though. He would torment her. There were stupid things he would do to make life difficult for her. Like removing the home telephone and taking it to work with him so she couldn't use it or withholding weekly housekeeping money so she couldn't buy groceries. She would have to go to the neighbours and work things out.

The way I saw it, he treated her no better than a slave. Who does that?

Who the hell taught him to treat her that way?

He was also good at using the silent treatment on her. I watched him doing it many, many times and it was something that I learnt to use as well later on in my life. He would block her out by refusing to talk to her and he also abused her. I heard it and sometimes even witnessed it.

What Is This Place: Heaven Or Hell?

One time, he caught me outside their bedroom door and boy did I pay for it.

He was careful with Mum, just as he was with me. He always spoke softly so no one else could hear and he always tried to do things when no one else was around. His abuse of her was awful and I, many times, wondered why she put up with it.

Little did I know that I would find out the 'why' for myself later on in my life.

> *INSIGHT: When you live with trauma, even emotional and mental abuse, you believe it is normal. How crazy is that? I thought that Mum and Dad's relationship was normal. I thought that the way Dad treated me was normal. At that time, I had nothing to compare it to.*

Childhood was one blunder after another for me. Dad taught me that I had to navigate the expectations and orders of adults. From him, I learned how to behave and how to handle it. When Dad told me off, when I did something wrong, I was sent to my room.

Years later I would remember the space inside myself that I created. That was where I would retreat to, far away from the cruel and harsh outside world.

In that deep internal space was a North American Indian man with brown skin and long, dark hair. I would go to him whenever I was abused or in trouble. He never spoke; we just sat in silence together and his presence calmed me.

THE WORLD OF PRIMARY SCHOOL BEGINS

Primary school was something else for me. Now I had adults who were kind and were encouraging me to speak up; the total opposite of Dad at home.

This was so uncomfortable. I was embarrassed to have attention focused on me.

At home, this sort of attention meant being made an example of. I was so confused and painfully shy. Whenever the attention was upon me, I would go red in the face thinking I was being made an example of again.

The teachers were trying to help me, guiding me to learn and grow. It was so foreign to me, and my instant reaction was to feel threatened and anxious.

I loved swimming. I was really good at backstroke and swam in individual and relay races. I was placed into the competition; the first one was held at Harold Holt Memorial Pool.

I remember being so excited and I had the biggest butterflies. It went well and I came second in the individual.

It was during the relay that it happened…

There were certain words or phrases that Dad used that would trigger me. I heard him clearly from the sidelines and he got inside my head; I froze.

I never finished that race, and I never swam competition again.

After I recovered from my operation, I got to have some girls sleep over for my birthday. I was so excited because this had never happened before. It was rare for me to have any friends over during the day – let alone to sleep over.

THE SÉANCE

We were in the lounge room, all excited and in our pyjamas.

We decided to do a séance. We really had no idea what we were doing and, in the end, nothing happened except a lot of giggles. Mum called out from the kitchen and announced that the food was ready, and all my friends got up and ran from the room.

There were two ways to go to the kitchen from the lounge. One was through the dining room to the right or through the double glass doors to the left, into the hallway and then into the kitchen.

I was alone in the lounge, sitting on the floor. I was a bit disappointed that nothing had happened. It would have been so exciting for something to happen, especially at my birthday party. Oh well.

I got up and turned to leave through the double glass doors and there standing in front of me, was my Uncle Gordon.

Gordon had died recently.

He had drowned while trying to save my cousin Mark from drowning in the ocean. They had both died.

It was such a tragedy.

But there he was, standing in the doorway. I froze. He seemed nice and he felt friendly, but I was absolutely terrified. I actually ran through him, through the hallway and into the kitchen. I told everyone what had just happened. They all ran into the lounge, but he wasn't there.

No one believed me, nobody even cared that much. But I know what I saw.

Growing up, I absolutely idolised my Auntie Joy. She was Mum's youngest sister; always well dressed, with makeup and hair in place. She had a wonderful way about her and a wonderful way of speaking.

She could do no wrong in my eyes.

She was a hairdresser with her own salon and even travelled the world on a huge ship. I remember us all going to the docks to wave her goodbye. I decided that when I grew up, I was going to be just like her.

DREAMS ARE BROKEN

When I was about 13 years old, we had a BBQ at home. Friends and relatives were invited and that included my Auntie Joy.

I was about to have one of the defining moments in my life. You know the ones that are burned into your memory forever; you just never ever forget them.

What Is This Place: Heaven Or Hell?

Everyone was outside enjoying themselves. I went back into the house to get something from the kitchen. That's when I heard my mum and Auntie Joy in the dining room.

Auntie Joy was crying, so I stayed to listen. She was telling Mum that her marriage was a mess, that her life was a mess and that everything was falling apart.

I was absolutely shattered. Who was I going to be now when I grew up?

My dreams of the future disappeared.

Before I move on to high school, I want to share with you three very significant things that stuck with me about my dad:

1. He often, throughout my childhood, called me a *"Know All, Know Nothing"* and in my younger years, that comment really hurt. I saw it as a put-down. Later on in my life, I came to realise that it was also a very important phrase because fundamentally, as part of spiritual evolution, we strive to know all and know nothing.

I translated his statement into, *"You have no right to speak your mind or your truth!"*

2. He called me *"King of the Kids."* He did this anytime I had finished playing with the other neighbourhood kids. Again, in my younger years, that comment really hurt. Later in life, I could see that all my friends in the neighbourhood actually always came to me, met at my house and looked to me to figure out what we would do or what we would play.

I translated his statement into, *"You are not a leader, you don't deserve to be."*

3. There were many times when he would complain to Mum, *"She's looking at me like that again,"* or he would say, *"See, she's got that look on her face."* He wanted to smack that look off my face sometimes. It often confused me because firstly, I couldn't see the look on my face and, secondly, I really had no idea exactly what he was referring to. What I did know was that look triggered him somehow; he didn't like it. I eventually discovered what that was all about, and I will reveal it to you later on in this book.

I translated his statement into, *"Whenever I see or feel someone else getting uncomfortable when I talk to them; it's your fault and you have to stop talking or withdraw completely."*

THE TRAUMA OF HIGH SCHOOL

High school was next. It was another one of life's exciting and nervous moments.

Our grade 6 teacher told us again and again that we were going to be small fish in a big ocean. Not very comforting.

However, I loved it; it was such an adventure. New buildings, new corridors, new people, new teachers. I loved it all.

I quickly made friends and we all ended up being friends right throughout high school. There was a group of about 14 of us. We spent breaks together, lunch times together and eventually, went to parties and outings together.

I loved sewing, music and cooking and even took up ballroom dancing classes. I didn't like sports or anything that involved competition.

Harold Holt Memorial Pool had put an end to anything like that.

I learned that I could master anything I put my mind to, but I had no idea what I wanted to be.

Emotionally, I struggled. I was still blushing at times when I had to stand in front of the class or became the focus of attention, of course, anytime the attention was on me.

As long as I could remain invisible, as long as no one singled me out, as long as I wasn't the centre of attention; I was good.

Terribly unrealistic expectations really.

Chapter 2

THE RELATIONSHIPS THAT SHAPED ME

I struggled with relationships.

The significant relationships up until high school were with Mum and Dad and, of course, there were the holidays spent with Nan and Pop. They were the only adults that I had spent significant time with. With other adults, I would only get bits and pieces of their behaviour, so they didn't count. What I had figured out though, was that there was no intimacy or closeness in our family.

Up until high school, I had learned from my mum that it was best to shut up and get on with it. From my dad, I learned that I would never amount to much. During primary school, I had three good friends (Debra, Kathy and Sandra) but of course, we weren't talking about insecurities and problems then. Primary school was for learning and having fun.

My Auntie Win was special to me. She was on my side; she was kind to me, filled with so much wisdom and was beautiful to be around. She showed me love and gave me gifts from time to time. She helped me get my ears pierced when Mum and Dad wouldn't, gave me my first pair of pale purple stockings and a crazy-looking witch flying on a broomstick. It was a mobile toy that hung from the ceiling. She also gave me a fine gold chain with a cross on it; I loved it.

I watched relationships at school – especially the ones between girls and boys. I was trying to figure out how they happened; I just didn't have a clue.

Here was my problem… I couldn't work out how people moved from sitting next to each other and having a laugh to holding hands and being in a relationship. I became an intense observer and was frightened of any boy paying me attention and catching me out; like finding out I really didn't know what to do.

My insecurities were taking over and it never occurred to me that one of these boys would be interested in me. I didn't even realise when one of them was genuinely interested in me.

DARREN

As a group, we would hang out together at someone's home. These were always during the day because I wasn't allowed out at night.

I remember Darren James. He liked me and I liked him. We all went to the movies one day and he asked me if I wanted to go. I agreed. Was that a date?

I had no idea because we were all going together.

We sat next to each other, and he held my hand. Did I mention that the movie was *The Exorcist*?

It was the scariest thing I had ever seen and I'm sure I left my fingerprints imbedded in his hand.

Looking back, I think he was about as insecure as me. The problem was he never declared anything to me, but I did see the way he looked at me from time to time. I was never going to declare anything to him – just in case I was wrong. We got on really well, but it never became anything else.

This leads me to a very funny story in the future that I must tell.

Darren became a radio announcer on *3AW*. I was a conveyancer at a law firm. This is about 2018, I think. One of my clients came into the office to return some paperwork. As she went to leave, she stopped me and asked, *"Do you listen to Darren James on 3AW?"*

I told her I didn't.

She said, *"I was listening to his show the past weekend and the theme was something to do with 'that first lost love' and Darren had spoken about his and said her name was Helen Taylor."*

She looked at me again and asked, *"Are you that Helen Taylor?"*

I was amazed. Yes, I was *that* Helen Taylor.

Fancy that? All these years later to find out that I was his first lost love. If only one of us had been a little braver.

This made me think about something else at that time. What greater power is there that arranges the coincidence of me having that particular conveyancing client at that particular time that she listened religiously to *3AW* and that she could relay the message?

What makes things like that happen?

Back to my story, I missed the boat with Darren.

Looking back, I think Dad's poison was at work again. You see Darren and Michael C were two respectful boys; they were different from the other boys in our group. The others were the ones who got into smoking and bad behaviour that got them into trouble – they were the ones who used alcohol and experimented with sex. Darren and Michael didn't.

Already, I was on the path of seeking out the 'bad boys'.

ANDREW

Soon after, I met Andrew. He worked at the chemist in the shopping centre across from the school. He would take me to the church across from the school on a Friday night – it opened up a space for young kids to come and meet. There was music and a really nice atmosphere and tables and chairs so you could sit down and chat.

He was respectful, Christian, lovely and kind and, I didn't realise until a lot later in my life, looked very much like the spirit guide I had when I was a child. He went to the tech school down the road and was working at the chemist to save up money to follow his dream of going to Antarctica and exploring.

I really liked him and loved that he knew what he wanted and was going to make it happen.

He had beautiful, long, dark hair and had such a gentle way about him. He had all the time in the world for me and always walked me home because it was dark. He would kiss me on the cheek to say goodbye and tell me he would see me soon. And he did.

We met up a few times after that and then he told me his dream was about to come true. He had saved enough money and had booked his ticket on the boat to Antarctica. He walked me home one final time and kissed me goodbye.

Andrew showed me how to have a vision and go after it. He inspired me.

I never saw him again.

BOYS AND ALCOHOL

At 16, I was allowed to go to a party at the house of one of my friends; everyone would be there. The rest of my friends had already been doing this on a regular basis. For me, this would be my first time at a party. I was so excited.

I got myself ready, put on a bit of makeup, collected some of my favourite record albums to take with me and let Dad know I was ready to go.

Immediately, he started at me with his poison. He told me I looked ridiculous with all the makeup and that I looked like a prostitute. He continued with his poison the whole way there in the car.

I got out and agreed with Dad that he would pick me up at 11.00pm.

The party was great. Someone had brought along alcohol and some of the boys made the girls a *Bacardi* and coke each. It tasted nice.

The music started and we were all dancing and sipping away at our drinks. Little did I know, but the boys thought it was really funny to keep topping our drinks up with the *Bacardi*. That meant that at some stage we were drinking something that was mostly *Bacardi* and very little coke.

We were getting very drunk. I had never been drunk before.

As the night wore on and inhibitions were being thrown to the wind; couples were disappearing off into the bedrooms. I certainly threw caution to the wind and ended up in a bedroom with one of the boys.

This was my first time with foreplay. Finally! It was good that he knew what he was doing because I was pretty awkward at first. It didn't matter and it was actually nothing like I had imagined. It was pretty nice.

We went back out into the party. Someone announced that my dad was outside in his car.

"Oh my god," I thought as I realised how drunk I was. *"How did I get this drunk?"*

I could hardly walk properly.

I gathered up my bag and the stack of records I had brought along. I took a deep breath, stepped out the front door and tried to walk properly to Dad's car.

I couldn't – I stumbled and fell over, records went everywhere. I got the silent treatment all the way home.

The silent treatment was just as poisonous as his words. Neither Mum nor Dad believed my story about only having a couple of drinks.

It wasn't until the next week at school that I found out how we got so drunk. The story of 'topping up' our glasses was doing the rounds, and everyone thought it was hysterical.

In forms 5 and 6 (years 11 and 12), there were many more parties and a few more encounters with foreplay but I never actually had a boyfriend.

Many times in my life, I would experience people projecting on me. People who thought they knew what I was thinking or what I was doing. Most of the time, they were wrong.

I remember sitting around with my girlfriends one afternoon and Sue, decided to match a song title with each one of us.

She gave me, *"If you can't be with the one you love, love the one you're with."*

It gave me insight into what she thought of me. I was so misunderstood. I was trying to figure it all out.

It was at a big birthday party for Kyle's 18th (he was one of our group at school) that I lost my virginity.

Everyone was there; all my friends from school, Kyle's family and their friends. It was huge. I had a couple of drinks and remember looking around the room.

I came upon a really nice-looking guy; he was a friend of Kyle's that I had never met before. I decided that I was going to lose my virginity that night and it was going to be with him. I zoned in on him and made it happen.

It was done and I still remember thinking the strangest thing… It wasn't painful and there was no bleeding. That's what all my girlfriends had spoken of.

Why didn't that happen to me?

TIME TO LEAVE SCHOOL

Towards the end of high school, we were all encouraged to think about what we were going to do once we left school. Towards the end of form 4, we were all encouraged to select subjects for form 5 and 6 –subjects that reflected what we wanted to be or do after high school.

I spoke with the school counsellor who was there to help us figure it all out. I told him I wanted to be a hairdresser or a beauty therapist. Hairdressing was a four-year apprenticeship and beauty therapy wasn't available in Victoria.

I would have to live for 12 months in Sydney to actually get the appropriate training. I didn't know what to do, so I was encouraged to focus on secretarial studies and I also chose legal studies.

I left school and worked at the local newsagent while I was looking for a hairdressing job. I even did a TV interview on a morning TV show that was set up to support job seekers. It was with *Channel 9* in Bendigo Street, Richmond.

I was so nervous, but I did it and remembered that the whole neighbourhood knew it was happening and everyone got up at 6.00am in the morning to watch me. It got me a call from *Mary Kay Cosmetics,* but I did nothing about it.

They were a network marketing company, and I just didn't have the confidence to take that step.

Something in the universe had shifted and I found a hairdressing job. It was with *Robert Hartley Hairdressing* in Heidelberg.

I started my apprenticeship and the first thing I had to do was change my name. They already had a hairdresser working for them called Helen. It was explained that when the place got busy people would be regularly calling out my name to do a shampoo, rinse a colour, sweep up the floor and it became confusing if two people had the same name.

I chose Linda. Linda was a friend of mine, so it made sense to me that I would answer to that name.

Two significant things happened while I was in hairdressing.

I got dermatitis on my hands. My hands were dry, red and the skin was cracking between the fingers. It was very painful and difficult to manage.

I got to be a model on stage at a hair show. They loved my incredibly curly hair, and it was perfect for one of their new hairstyles. The show was at a venue called Leonda in Hawthorn and was hosted by Issi Dye – who, at that time, was a popular TV show host and performer. I was starstruck.

Backstage, I got quick instructions on how to walk the catwalk and off I went.

Lights, camera, action. It was incredible.

BROKEN DREAMS BUT MOVING ON

Shortly after that, I finished up with *Robert Hartley*. It just wasn't working out. My hands were getting worse and constant water, shampoos and hair dyes were only making them crack and bleed even more.

I was not destined to be a hairdresser.

I was devastated. That dream was shattered. Now what was I going to do?

I didn't have a clue. While I was unemployed, everyone encouraged me to do what was expected – go on the dole or, *"Just get any job, anything, a checkout job at Coles."*

For some reason, I knew that if I did that, I would begin to walk a different path in life and I wanted more than that. I 'knew' that I could not just take anything.

Something would come along that was right for me.

It's really hard to hold onto that 'knowing' when the people around you just think you are lazy or useless.

Dad hated that I wasn't working. Mum was the one saying, *"Just get a checkout job, get anything."*

My waiting paid off and I started my first job in the legal field. I was a clerk and typist for *Coady Dwyer* in St Kilda Road. It was wonderful.

I started from the ground up; firstly, as a clerk going into the city on a regular basis and learning how to file documents at the County Court and Supreme Court, how to sort out stamping at the State Revenue Office and lodging and searches at the Land Titles Office.

I loved it. I also loved that I found the most amazing knitwear shop that created one-off thigh length jumpers that I absolutely loved to wear when I went out clubbing.

I would wear them with skinny jeans and pixie boots. I have no excuses for the fashion of the 80s!

I quickly went up the ranks and was trained in *Word Processing* – the amazing new invention of the times. I became part of the 'typing pool' typing up all court documents, letters, wills etc.

Soon, I went a step further to being the fill in secretary to Mr Coady himself.

Keep me filled with adventure and learning new things and I was at my happiest. I would come to understand later in my life that if I wasn't learning and doing something new; I would create trouble. You'll see…

It was at *Coady Dwyer* that I met Kerryn. We 'clicked' immediately and started driving in to work together on a regular basis. We swapped each week as the designated driver and actually had exactly the same car; a *Mazda 1300*.

Mine was called Fate and I called myself and anyone who drove in the car with me, the Fatalistics.

Fate took me wherever I needed to go. That was my slogan. And, by the way, the registration number was *'LVE 302'*. Fancy that?

Kerryn was a bit of a hippie. She lived with her boyfriend in a house in Surrey Hills and I would stay for a cuppa sometimes after work. I loved her independence; her style of living.

I had never come across anyone like her up to now. She drank herbal teas, burned incense and knew stuff about massage.

She gave me a foot massage one day; it was incredible. I remember wondering how come I had no idea these sorts of things existed.

Little did I know, Kerryn was setting the scene for me to learn massage some 15 years later.

Chapter 3

THE POTENTIAL

NOEL

It was around the same time after meeting Kerryn that I met Noel. However, before I get into him, let me explain the set-up of my social scene at the time.

My best friends were Kerry and Jan – we had been friends from high school. Kerry loved going out and dancing just as much as I did. It was 1980; nightclubs and discos were everywhere.

We squeezed ourselves into the tightest jeans you could imagine. I remember the three of us laughing one night as Jan got dressed. She lay down on her bed with a metal clothes hanger hooked in the zip of her jeans. It was the only way she could pull the zipper all the way up. Then she had to get herself off the bed and stand up. It was hysterical.

We went to the *Croydon Hotel* on a Tuesday night, dancing and drinking the night away and either football club discos or clubs on a Friday and Saturday night.

Kerry was a man magnet. She always wore one-piece jumpsuits with a zip at the front that got lower and lower as the night went on. She was never without a boyfriend.

Me, on the other hand, still had insecurities. Or did I?

I just never really saw the point of having a boyfriend. One-night stands were much better —no attachment, no awkwardness, no commitment.

I loved dancing though. I didn't realise at the time, but it was a form of therapy for me. When I danced, I forgot about everything else in the world.

Peta and Gail were also my friends, and I would often see them at the *Croydon Hotel*. It was through them that I was invited away for a camping trip to Eildon and that's where I met Noel and the many other people who were a part of his world.

He was six years older than me; lived in a sprawling blue stone home with his parents and had his own wing of the home. He had everything; that's how I saw him.

The family had money; his parents and two brothers were all part of the family landscaping business, and they were all very successful.

Going out with Noel opened up a completely new world for me. He showed me adventure… Fast cars, camping, jet skis, boating, snow skiing, parties, different music… A whole other way of life that was truly inspiring.

LOVE, DRUGS AND FAST CARS

We went to Bathurst for the annual car race and we drove there in his *Torona SLR 5000*. He challenged me to learn how to roll joints. If he was going to drive the whole way to Bathurst; I had to roll us joints along the way. Seemed like a fair deal to me.

I had a pack of rolling papers and a pack of tobacco, and I rolled and rolled until I got it right.

Bathurst was amazing. We camped there along with hundreds of other people and everyone was smoking dope. It was a whole new thing for me, so I eased myself into it.

A lot of Noel's friends were also on the mountain and we visited some of them who were all together in a large tent. They were smoking dope and making lunch; toasted sandwiches. I remember the tent was a haze of smoke and I had a few puffs of a joint.

The tent was really warm and relaxing, and I started to feel a little strange. The man making the toasted sandwiches asked me, *"What do you want on your sandwich, Helen?"*

I couldn't speak, I just stood there. He asked me again. I still couldn't speak.

Let me try and explain what was happening to me… I was having an out-of-body experience.

My body was standing there but I was somewhere else, kind of watching me and him. I knew I wanted to say, *"Ham and cheese, please,"* but I couldn't connect with my body.

He asked me again and, all of a sudden, I was back in my body and told him, *"Ham and cheese, please."*

Wow! That had never happened to me before. It was such a crazy feeling.

Through Noel, I met a lot of new people, older more mature people, and a lot of the time, they triggered my own insecurities. I would feel like an imposter, a child.

At parties, the others would be having conversations about things I either hadn't experienced or didn't know a lot about. One friend of his asked me to be a model. He was a photographer and was doing a shoot for a boat company. He needed a model in a bikini to take some of the boating shots.

That was a big trigger; I said no.

A group of us were all sitting around a large table having a few drinks and some food one afternoon. I sat back in my chair only to glimpse my friend Gail playing footsies with Noel under the table. He wasn't reacting but he also wasn't pulling his feet away – major trigger.

My insecurities were starting to grow and the bigger they got; the bigger the gap between me and Noel grew. This played out dramatically in our last night together. It was a night filled with one disaster after another.

The Potential

We were at a party at Dave's house; one of Noel's best friends. Everyone was staying over. There were sleeping bags and makeshift beds all over the lounge room floor.

There was a lot of drinking, dancing and fun. During the night, I went down the hallway to find the toilet. Noel's brother Chris was drunk, and he grabbed me, pulled me into a bedroom and kissed me. This just managed to happen as his wife was walking down the hall… Of course.

Within seconds, the whole party knew about it and people were quick to jump to conclusions. How did it all become my fault? The party quickly became very uncomfortable.

Fast forward to everyone getting ready to sleep. I walked into the lounge to set up my sleeping bag next to Noel's only to find that Gail had already set hers up right next to his and she was just slipping into her sleeping bag.

I was triggered.

I was furious.

I went over and grabbed her and started pulling her and her sleeping bag out of the way. Problem was that she didn't have any clothes on; she was completely naked. Again… How did all of that become my fault? Clearly, she was making a move. Why the hell was she naked?

I didn't get much sleep that night.

SUICIDE WILL STOP THE PAIN

Noel drove me home the next morning. We drove in total silence. Simply he said, *"This is goodbye. We are over."*

I got out of the car. Devastated, I got to the front door and, as soon as I was inside, I started to cry. Big mistake: I was not home alone. Dad was home and immediately zeros in on me.

I tell him to leave me alone. He's like a vulture; he smells blood.

I go to my room to unpack but he followed me, picking and picking at me. I told him Noel and I broke up. He started at me again; he's found the wound.

He lets lose like the quiet assassin he is, absolutely relentless, *"Oh, he finally woke up to you, he realised you're a slut, realised you're worthless, a liar, useless, an embarrassment…"*

He is disgusting, ruthless, verbally attacking me and following me around the house; he just wouldn't let up.

I was broken, I couldn't handle it anymore, so I go out the backdoor to get away from him. I stood at the bottom of the back stairs wracked with tears and sobbing my heart out.

He stopped at the top of the stairs, watched me and, just when I thought he'd finished, he declared, *"I should have put that pillow over your head. I should have killed you when you were born."*

What did he just say?

The Potential

I stare at him horrified. He said, *"I had the chance you know, I wanted to. I should have put that pillow over your face."*

He seemed satisfied now. He smiled at me and went back into the house leaving me standing outside.

I couldn't breathe, I was paralysed.

His words had totally overwhelmed me. I stopped crying and my mind was empty. His words were just too much.

I heard him get his car keys, the front door slam, start his car and leave.

I was alone and I realised that he was right. He should have killed me.

I wiped my eyes and headed back into the house. I went straight to the medicine cabinet and grabbed all the prescription drugs I could see.

Like a robot, numb and mechanical, I started eating the pills.

"He's right, I should be dead," I said to myself.

I ate all the pills, one bottle after another. I walked into the hallway and sat down on the floor.

I felt better; totally numb.

IS THERE SOMETHING THAT LOOKS OUT FOR US?

Then the phone rang. I had no idea how much time had passed. I couldn't get up, the room was fuzzy, so I crawled over to the phone.

It was my friend Peta. She asked, *"Is that you, Helen?"*

"Why would she ask me that?" I thought. *"Of course, it's me."*

She asked if I was okay. *"Of course, I was okay!"* I thought.

She was at Gail's place and said they were worried about me. I told her I was fine. She said that was great and that they were coming around to see me and to wait for them, they would only be a few minutes.

She hung up.

Next thing, they were both at my front door which just happened to be unlocked. They wanted me to come for a drive with them. They grabbed my bag and put me into the car.

I remember it was such a beautiful day, warm with a totally blue sky.

Now I was at Box Hill Hospital sitting in a cubicle in emergency. They wanted to know what I'd taken and how much I'd taken. They pumped my stomach and wanted me to stay overnight.

I discharged myself.

That night at home, I was greeted with such *overwhelming* love from my parents (hint of sarcasm here):

"How dare you do that! Don't you ever do that again," said Dad.

Mum added, *"Are you okay now?"*

I replied defiantly, *"Yes."*

"Good, that's good. Well, I better go and get dinner ready then."

Conversation over.

I had many questions after what I had just been through.

First one being… Why didn't I die?

I knew something weird had just taken place. You see, Peta was a registered nurse, she could tell immediately that something was wrong with me. Fancy her being the one to call at that exact moment? Little did I know at the time, but more strange things were going to happen to me further down the track.

LIFE AFTER NOEL

Life continued on without Noel. I began to grow apart from Kerry and Jan as friends. They were both into finding a man, settling down sort of stuff and that just wasn't something I was interested in.

I met Linda through Kerry and we got on straight away. She worked in retail as a salesperson and didn't aspire to much more than that. She could be super critical of people and life and wore that as a badge. She loved pushing people's buttons and getting reactions.

She hated life and figured she had just been dealt a crappy hand.

I had loved her 'I don't give a shit' attitude and have to say, I took some of that on board. I also became pretty caustic when I wanted. Up to this point in my life, I had pretty much followed the pack. I had been shy and introverted, but all that was changing.

Linda helped and drugs certainly helped.

I felt better around her. Don't get me wrong; I wasn't doing that consciously, but I think she was more broken than me and that made me feel better. She didn't want much out of life and was happy to do whatever I wanted to do.

That was perfect because I had decided that I didn't want relationships with men – that was just too hard. I vowed to remain single; it was easier. All I wanted was one-night stands, the dance floor and drugs.

Smoking dope now and then with Noel had now turned into joints, bongs and the occasional night of speed. Linda smoked bongs and knew how to score speed which was a known amphetamine.

We would go out a few nights a week. We'd snort some speed before going out, drink lots of alcohol, I would hit the dance floor (I just loved dancing and loosing myself on the dance floor), Linda hated dancing, so she would pick up some guy, go back to his place and have sex – then we'd go back to Linda's, hit some bongs to wind down, go home, go to sleep, get up the next morning, go to work and repeat.

WORK HARD, PLAY HARD

I had moved on from *Coady Dwyer* by this time and had decided that I didn't really like the politics of working in a large firm, so I started working for a sole practitioner, Peter in North Balwyn. I could learn more in a smaller environment and was given a wider scope of things to learn and do.

Remember a sense of adventure and learning was always important to me. I needed it as much as I needed air.

Peter didn't know it at that time, but he was about to go on a rollercoaster of experiences with me. Lucky him!

It's important to me at this time to let you know about me and drugs. I could take or leave drugs at this time of my life. I certainly used them whenever I was going out, but I didn't need them every day. I want to be clear about this.

Linda, on the other hand, had a problem. She couldn't stop them.

I loved working for Peter. I learnt all about conveyancing and debt collection. I even got to 'instruct' a couple of times with him in the Magistrates Court and Supreme Court. I was so happy learning and mastering all sorts of things and those opportunities just didn't present themselves in a larger firm.

I got to know more about Peter personally, got to know his wife and kids and he got to know more about me, as well. Peter's business grew – he was making good connections in the insurance industry and taking on more work – predominately insurance claims.

We moved office to South Melbourne to be closer to the major insurance firm that was now his biggest client.

It was fabulous. This was the 1980s and South Melbourne was an inner-city suburb filled with businesses and pubs.

We had moved into what had previously been a brothel in Moray Street. It was a single fronted premises with white painted walls, black lacquered architraves and mouldings and plush red carpet.

Pretty crazy stuff for a legal practice.

It was standard practice to go to lunch at the pub on Fridays, eat and drink plenty and leave late into the night. Lunches were ways of doing business and getting to know clients.

I would often finish up at the office and make my way to the pub to join Peter and the business associates. This was also a time when it was standard practice to smoke in pubs and in the office. I always had an ashtray on my desk.

It seems so surreal now looking back at those times, because so much of what we did then would seem so unacceptable now.

Chapter 4

I THINK I MET MY DAD

GREG

I was 22 years old. My life was pretty good. Every now and then, one of my one-night stands would get attached and want a relationship. I would entertain that for a bit, but it never lasted long. I just didn't want them to.

Along the way though, I met Erica. She was a neighbour of one of my longer-term partners. We would catch up from time to time and then she got a boyfriend, and then she got engaged and, because all of this was making her so happy, she decided that I should find someone and be just as happy as her.

Bless her; she really thought she had it all figured out for me.

My Return To Love

Erica and her fiancé Rob set me up on a blind date with a guy named Greg. We went to a pub in South Melbourne one Friday afternoon and, after a few drinks, we were all getting along and having a fabulous time.

Greg was intriguing. He lived in Portland and worked at *Dalgety's* taking care of the docks, wharfies and ships – and he was also very good looking.

He swept me off my feet. Within hours, he had convinced me to come with him to Portland and spend the weekend. Why not?

I told no-one and we headed off on the four-hour drive to his place.

> *INSIGHT: During the afternoon at the pub, a woman walked in the front door. She was 'mutton dressed up as lamb' as the saying goes. What I mean by that is… She was an older woman trying to dress 20 years younger and it didn't work that well. Anyway, I happened to point her out and said, "Have a look at what just walked in," and Greg immediately waved at the woman and said, "Oh, my mum's here." He got her attention and waved for her to come over. It was a classic case of me putting my foot in my mouth, but it was also so funny. Imagine that; it was his mum. It should have been a warning sign for me then, but I didn't see it.*

Greg and I had a fabulous weekend of conversation, sightseeing and intimacy. He was the perfect gentleman and went to great lengths to take care of me.

I had never had a man look at me as though I was the only thing in the world. It was wonderful.

As the weekend came to a close, he booked me a flight from Portland to Melbourne on a small aircraft and made sure all arrangements were made to get me back home safely.

I was hooked.

GREG WAS MY NEW DRUG

Greg had now become my focus. I didn't see Linda as much anymore. Her and the drugs moved into the background.

Greg and I saw each other every fortnight. He would come down to Melbourne for the weekend and then it was my turn to go to Portland for the weekend. I loved driving; so, every weekend, when it was my turn, I would leave Melbourne as soon as I finished work at 5.00pm, have my music cassettes set up to play along the way and, four hours later, I would be at his doorstep. I would spend the weekend and then 5.00am on the Monday morning, I would drive all the way back to Melbourne and arrive at work for 9.00am.

I just loved getting away from my family, getting away from Melbourne. I felt fulfilled, with a purpose; I felt alive and I was in love.

Greg loved the ocean, surfing, competition, Mexican food and people. He opened up a whole new world to me. We were always sightseeing or socialising. Initially, he lived in a shared house with two nurses. That triggered me a bit but, when I met the girls, I could see they were no threat to me, and I was happy again.

Every other weekend when I didn't see Greg, I began to catch up with Linda again and, through her, met a new group of friends including Gina, Jeanette, Chris and Dave. They were the best friends you could have, and they didn't do drugs; so, Linda just kept doing drugs on her own.

There was one girl that became part of Greg's group of friends in Portland, her name was Julie, and I could see that even though she was in a relationship, she liked Greg. Greg was a little like I was in the naive department sometimes. He couldn't see it at all.

Never mind, I'd tell myself; just move on. I'm the one going out with him, so I made the best of it.

I felt so inspired with Greg. We were always doing new things and trying new things and then, he mentioned going to America and asked me if I would go with him.

Not in my wildest dreams had I ever thought of going overseas.

He had never met his father. His mother split from him before he was born. He had done some research and found some of his father's family in the US and wanted to go and see if he could find him and meet him.

I agreed to go as long as it was also going to be a holiday and having fun, as well.

I was so excited.

THE NIGHTMARE OF GREG

We booked all the flights and accommodation before we left: San Francisco, Seattle, Chicago, New York, Miami, New Orleans, Memphis, St Louis, Las Vegas, San Diego, Los Angeles and Honolulu, before coming back home.

Seattle and St Louis were places where Greg had found family contacts; they were a 'must visit', whereas the rest was vacation time.

It was July 1983. We spent just over a month travelling the States. It looked a little like this…

The Golden Gate Bridge, Palace of the Fine Arts, Alcatraz and the Red Wood Forests, Space Needle Seattle, then Chicago. I had no idea that there was a prison built smack in the middle of Chicago and it was shaped like a triangle. The city was pretty scary initially.

There were five separate locks on the motel room door and every person I saw was black. Not one white person. That was pretty confronting. It's just a crazy feeling to see so many people of a different colour – only because you are just not used to it. I loved the Windy City.

New York was fabulous. We settled into our hotel and stepped back out onto the street.

Immediately, a man raced past followed by two police officers with their guns drawn. I ran after them – I mean c'mon, this was New York! Greg was yelling after me to stop but I took no notice. The cops chased the man into a car park, caught him and arrested him. I felt like I was in one of those cop shows on TV, it was so exciting.

We went to Miami because we had to go to Disney World. We went on ride after ride including Space Mountain. We visited the Elvis Presley Mansion. I couldn't believe that, after all these years, there were still people standing around his memorial crying. I remember thinking to myself that people really need to get over it – he's been gone a long time.

Las Vegas was hot and filled with so many bright lights that made it even hotter. The Eagles were playing an outdoor arena at one of the clubs but were booked out. We got a drink, relaxed in banana lounges around the adjacent pool and got to hear the whole concert anyway. How cool was that?

San Diego Zoo was a hit. Magic Mountain in Los Angeles, at that particular time, had the tallest roller coaster in the world and, of course, I had to go on it. And, also being in California, I definitely had to hire and drive a convertible.

Unfortunately, after riding the unique high that comes with travelling, it was in Los Angeles that trouble struck and the high crashed.

HE HIT ME

Greg had been going through all sorts of emotions and anxieties through this trip. He was getting pretty wound up, but I wasn't going to let it ruin my holiday. We hired the convertible and, because it was my dream, I was the driver.

We set off on the highway and I was busy navigating a new car, a big car, the six-lane highway and driving on the wrong side of the road.

Forgive me if I said something wrong, because to this day, I can't recall what I said. Whatever it was, it triggered Greg and he smacked me in the mouth with the back of his hand. It was actually his watch that hit me in the mouth.

I immediately lost two teeth and started bleeding.

Within seconds, a police car was behind us, siren on, lights flashing, so I pulled over.

Now, here's the kicker.

The police got out and came over to me. They said they noticed me driving erratically and wanted to know why. I told them we are from Australia, and I was new to driving here, I miscalculated the traffic, had to brake suddenly and smacked myself into the steering wheel.

Can you believe that?

Instantly I made it all my fault. They were very understanding and suggested I follow them to the nearest dental hospital, which I did. The dentist stopped the bleeding and patched things up so we could get on our way.

Greg was all apologetic but made it all about not being able to find his father, said that I just didn't understand… Blah blah blah.

Next was Honolulu. It was stunning. Sunbathing at the beach – if you remember the TV series *Gilligan's Island*, it was the same spot that their boat launched from. We all love a story to tell when we get home, right?

We dined on a catamaran, road a dune buggy through the pineapple fields and tropical hills; it was so beautiful. We were so caught up in the magic of Honolulu that we got our departure dates mixed up, overstayed by one day and ended up sleeping on the beach for the last night. We didn't care; sleeping on the beach was an adventure.

As you have probably gathered, I locked away the whole event of being smacked in the mouth, buried it as deep as I possibly could.

I think I just weighed up all the good and positives things about our relationship against that one event and told myself it would never happen again and that it was just a one-off thing.

THE PORTLAND MOVE

In November of 1983, we got engaged and I moved to Portland to live with Greg. I was very excited about the move. I had a 'hope chest' or 'glory box' as they were called in those days.

It was a camphor chest full of all sorts of things to start a home. Cutlery, glassware, dinner set, towels, sheets, candles and picture frames. I got to open it up and start to use everything. I think the chest was also packed to the brim with my fantasies of setting up a home.

INSIGHT: Writing this part of the book brought up so many things. I came so close to death so many times. It brushed past me and made sure that I knew it was around. More times of being so terrified, so afraid, that I have buried under being so proud and tough and strong.

You know I had to push through these old feelings before I could begin to tell the rest of this story.

The trauma has resurfaced. I have allowed it to, I have felt it, I have screamed it out loud, it has wracked my heart with sobs and cries of anguish. I have cried until I broke, once again, letting the past loose. I had no idea what tremendous, powerful pain I had been carrying around for so long.

It didn't take long. I want to reassure you. When you truly let the past out, it is powerful, it is overwhelming, but it takes only moments, harsh, relentless moments to release itself and be gone; to be gone for good.

It will take you over. You will lose control. You must, it must; it's the only way it can happen.

It's an even playing field. No one person's trauma is any bigger or less than anyone else. It is ALL trauma, and we must let our hearts release and heal.

We must thank our hearts for the beautiful job they are doing for us every moment of every day.

I finished up with *Peter Fraser* in South Melbourne and started work with *William Bassett* and his small legal practice in Portland. Country life was very different and a lot slower. We both worked during the week and spent the weekends camping, taking drives and socialising. All seemed good for a while, then the wheels began to fall off.

It started with the 'pizza incident'. I had invited my friend Linda up for the weekend to stay with us and, on the Saturday, Greg went off to the Surf Club as he always did. He would spend hours paddle boarding and whatever other 'surfing' things he did. So, Linda and I did a bit of shopping and decided to make pizzas for the three of us for lunch.

We made two pizzas. Linda and I ate ours because Linda was getting hungry, and I had no idea how much longer Greg would be. It was delicious. Linda asked if she could have one more slice from the second pizza. Sure, she could. We made a joke about rearranging the slices to make it look like it was still a whole pizza.

Greg got home and got stuck into his pizza. He made a comment about there being a missing slice and he wanted to know where it was. Linda and I broke into laughter, remembering the silly joke we had shared earlier.

We weren't laughing at Greg and, after all, we were only talking about *one* slice of pizza here.

Greg asked to talk to me alone. He led me into the laundry and quietly and forcefully slammed me up against the laundry wall. It took me by complete surprise; I had no idea what was going on. He was furious about the missing slice of the pizza and being the subject of some sort of joke.

My whole back hurt. I had to think over what had just happened.

Something wasn't quite right with Greg. It was something I just couldn't put my finger on.

He was okay with me as long as I was doing what he thought was best for both of us. I had stopped seeing my friends; I had stopped going out with them. Now I had stopped seeing my family.

He was the centre of my world.

UNDERCOVER PSYCHO

I hadn't seen it before because I was happy to just focus on him. It was subtle, very subtle. Slowly and surely, he had pulled me away from everything and everyone I knew. I thought I had made all the choices myself, but I had made them because, when I didn't do what he wanted, something awful used to simmer up inside him and I could feel it.

Problem was I didn't want to address it. How could I address it?

Twice now I had seen him snap and I didn't want to see it again. So, I stayed quiet, even withdrew a little. I had no idea what to do.

His mother and sister came to visit. It was nice to see them. I stole a moment with his mum when I could and mentioned his behaviour to her and, to my astonishment, she acknowledged it.

She said, *"Yes, of course."*

She was surprised that there hadn't been more episodes; it was common for him to 'lose it' as far as she was concerned.

My Return To Love

What was I to do?

You can't negotiate with irrational behaviour; I had already learned that from my dad. Greg was looking more and more like a nutjob to me.

It came to a head one night when he was going to bed. I went into the spare bedroom to read for a while as I wasn't ready to go to sleep yet. He came into the spare room and asked why I was in the spare room. I said I was going to read for a while and I would do it here so I could have the light on and not disturb him.

He declared, *"If you fall asleep, I will wake you with a bucket of cold water!"*

What?!

That was a crazy thing to say. I assured him that I was going to read and had every intention of coming to bed.

So, guess what… You already guessed it. I fell asleep and was woken by a full bucket of cold water thrown over me and the bed I was lying on.

That was it for me. I was done. I rang my brother the next day and said I had to get out of Portland.

The following Saturday, while Greg was at the Surf Club, my brother and a couple of his friends came to the house with a trailer, we loaded it up and I left.

Why did I do it this way?

Because I was afraid.

I was afraid of Greg and the rage inside of him. He didn't stop there of course; he haunted me and stalked me.

Thankfully, the four-hour distance between us didn't make that so easy for him and he eventually dropped away into the world of crazy people I once knew.

THE ESCAPE OF DRUGS AND DANCEFLOORS

I got my job back with Peter Fraser. Remember I said he was going to regret having me around at some point?

Well, here it comes.

I also reconnected back with my friends including Linda, Chris, David, Gina and Jeanette.

Personal relationships were overrated, and I declared to myself that one night stands were a much safer option. My life was solely about working during the week and partying on the weekends.

It was back to the dancefloors for me. When I was on a dancefloor, nothing else existed. It was the same thing with the drugs – especially the speed. This drug removed all inhibitions, made me absolutely fearless and full of so much genuine love.

I just loved everyone and everything while on it. I could just be myself and release any bottled-up stuff from inside of me.

Here was the problem though…

I started smoking joints and having bongs when I was going out with Noel. I wasn't addicted though – I could take it or leave it.

After Noel, I smoked joints and bongs with Linda and that's also when I started snorting speed. Drugs became a necessity for going out. I just couldn't go out unless I had some speed and, of course, dope was needed to come down at the end of night.

Then, I stopped all drugs. I didn't do drugs at all with Greg. Smoking cigarettes was the strongest thing I was into. Greg didn't like the smoking because he was a health nut; he was all about eating well and exercise. Pity that didn't also include having a healthy mind.

After Greg, well… I got back into drugs and the whole drug thing escalated. The snorting speed and smoking bongs just wasn't enough. You get used to certain levels of drugs and, after time, you need more and more.

A few people I got to know were injecting the speed. I saw them when we went to score. I was curious and, by now, you have probably figured out what curiosity does for me. It draws me in.

At first, watching someone 'shoot up' made me shudder. I thought of all the things that could go wrong but, like anything, once you hang around and see it again and again, you become desensitised, you start bargaining with yourself and rationalise it all out. You start to see more positives than negatives. You know what I mean?

So eventually, I let someone inject me.

Holy cow, what an experience. It's called a rush. You inject the speed straight into your bloodstream and it rushes immediately to the base of your skull. It lights up your brain and an enormous warmth rushes right through your entire body.

Your senses are immediately heightened and you're on high alert. It was incredible.

I knew I needed to get a handle on taking speed this way. I realised that if I had to rely on someone else to inject me, that was a good thing because I was in control of just how much I could take and how often.

I just loved taking speed. I could stay up for hours and hours, sometimes days and days, and I was seeing everything from a more heightened perspective. It was intoxicating to feel this way and I caught myself considering injecting myself.

That worried me so I said to myself that if I ever inject myself, I will cut my arm off.

WATCH WHAT YOU SAY OUT LOUD

Something listens to you when you make such clear declarations. Further on in my life, I have two other situations that totally prove what I just said. I will share these with you further on in the book.

So, I did it. I injected myself for the first time. I made sure I had someone with me so, if something went wrong, I had someone to take care of me. It was a big hurdle to jump but I did it. Problem was I just opened up a big door; I didn't know it at the time.

It was a door into a new reality where I was going to totally lose control.

Speed took over my life. I couldn't live without it.

My life used to revolve around working all week and partying all weekend. My life now revolved around getting speed, using speed and managing the comedowns.

Coming down was awful. Extreme tiredness, I would crash and sleep so deep that I wouldn't hear the phone or the doorbell. Nothing.

I didn't like coming down so I would do anything to avoid it. I was totally addicted to speed. It's like a virus though, it starts to affect every part of your life, little by little. I was always thinking about money, how to get more money, how to get more speed, how to watch my behaviour so people wouldn't always notice how high I was, watch how I dressed so people didn't see track marks on my arms.

I started being late for work, missing days here and there, making mistakes, falling asleep at the desk. I could start the day alright but, without any more speed, I would begin to fall apart by the afternoon.

Peter had moved his practice to the Preston Market. He had a major client there and we set ourselves up in the office suites to the side of the market. I was in charge of debt collection and also running the insurance files. If a mistake was made in either of these areas, it showed up pretty quickly.

Peter had a number of conversations with me; he was getting concerned.

But it all came to a head one day when I just didn't show up at all. No phone call, no nothing. He came around to my home, banged on the front door, rang me repeatedly and couldn't get an answer. I just didn't hear a thing; I was in a deep comedown sleep.

The following day, I arrived at work. He said, *"We're going for a drive."*

He shut the office and we drove a few hours into the country. He took me out for lunch and interrogated me because he was beside himself with worry and knew something was seriously wrong.

I opened up about everything and, when I was done, he declared, *"When we get back to the office, you are going to go home, you are going to tell your parents what's going on and if you don't, I will."*

I told Mum and Dad. It just confirmed for Dad what he already thought of me and Mum, it just made her more worried than she already was. The problem was though, they both had absolutely no idea how to handle the situation or what to do. They just let it slide.

I left Peter and started doing temp work. This meant working for an agency. The agency would have many short-term positions available each week at various different law firms. It was much easier to move around all the time, no-one saw me for long enough to get a handle on me or my behaviour.

I was good at anything I put my mind to. I could pick and choose when I worked and what jobs I wanted.

It was the time of *Duran Duran, Simple Minds, Spandau Ballet* and *Human League*, kind of a goth/romantic/dance era. I wore

My Return To Love

high collared shirts, lace tops, tight jeans and those pixie boots – yes, those boots were still around.

I worked only to get more money, to get more drugs. I hung around with 'goths' and anyone who was shooting up drugs. Needles were easy to come by as pharmacies sold them without question. Some of us even bought glass syringes and carried around a little kit of things with us at all times.

I was out of control but had no idea.

Chapter 5

I THINK I MET MYSELF

DAVID

I was 26 years old. I woke up one morning and something had changed, something had changed inside of me.

For some reason, over the coming weeks, I became totally consumed by the fact that I needed to find a man, get married and have kids.

I had never wanted this before.

I had never yearned for these things growing up, but now I was overtaken by these thoughts and feelings.

I had become a heat seeking missile; conditioning had kicked in. What I mean by that; the future me can now see clearly what was going on but, at the time, I had no idea why my focus had changed so dramatically.

Linda had met a couple of guys, but she was being secretive about them and, I could tell, she was trying to keep them separate from me. History told her that, when we met guys, I was usually the one to get lucky. I couldn't blame her really, but it just made me all the more determined to meet them.

Of course, it happened, it was always going to happen. We all met up and went out together. Me, Linda and the new guys she had met, Jeff and David. We all got on famously.

We were all into the same things: working and drugs.

I started going out with Jeff first but, unbeknown to me, David asked Jeff if he would step aside because he really had feelings for me and wanted to pursue them. Jeff did just that and David and I started going out together.

It was a much better fit. We got on really well.

> *INSIGHT: I got really stuck at this point of my story. It was extremely hard to go back, to remember and relive this time in my life. This was the start of a very important seven years in my life, but I had to go back and meet the version of me that felt so much guilt and shame about the drugs, the lifestyle and my behaviour.*
>
> *It was extremely hard to put the timeline in place. Drugs have created missing pieces which, through patience with me, have begun to emerge.*

David came with baggage. He had recently separated from his wife, and she took care of their two year old son. David was about as out of control as I was on drugs, so we were a good fit. We both jumped from job to job, anything to get money so we could keep up the supply of drugs. Work and party, work and party; that was the focus.

During the early days of us going out, I remember a time when we had to drop into my parents' house one evening. We arrived to find that only Dad was home. He was in a filthy mood and wasn't very happy to see us.

I had to collect something from one of the bedrooms and I came back to hear Dad questioning David about why he was going out with me. He was telling him disgusting things about me.

Bloody evil, awful things like, *"Did you know that she has slept with the whole football team?"* and other crazy nonsense.

What a psycho. I grabbed David and we left.

It was around this time that we moved into a terraced house together in North Fitzroy. We were doing so much speed. Now that I think of it; doing drugs and coming down would be filled with so many insecurities and paranoia.

How the hell did we even get to know each other?!

We were always doing speed or coming down. We got to see the highs and lows of each other, but rarely the reality.

It seemed that we were always navigating the next score or the next problem. Life was full of 'little fires' that we were always 'putting out'. But wasn't that just how life worked?

It seemed everyone else we knew was doing the same thing. We both just thought it was normal to be out of control a lot of the time.

Up to this point, we had both been working at various jobs/positions, moving around and making money. It wasn't easy holding down a job while doing so much speed. I was now working with a young, smart inner-city lawyer and David was working in sales with a big retail wholesaler.

He was really good at it, and they loved him. He was a good talker and could cast a spell with his words and me, I had such a confidence about me; I could nail any job I went for. I really wished I could have a job just doing interviews. I loved doing them, I was excellent at it.

BAGGAGE AND BURDENS

It was during this time that David's problems with his ex-wife started to escalate. She had diagnosed mental issues which were causing crazy and erratic behaviour. David was worried about her taking care of their son and her parents were making it clear that they wanted custody of the child.

It was messy.

I helped David navigate the application for custody and divorce. It was ugly stuff.

One day, during all of this other stuff going on, I had severe abdominal pains followed by a lot of blood clots, followed by a home visit by a GP who announced I had just miscarried.

I didn't even know I was pregnant. Curette revealed I had miscarried twins. Well, fancy that.

I just passed over all of that like it was a glitch in the system and continued on with life.

David's ex-wife was placed into psychiatric care; we saw her being driven away. Custody was shared between David and her parents, if I remember correctly. Her parents seemed determined to be the ones to raise the child.

Regular access to his son started and probably triggered something maternal in me which probably triggered a bit of common sense. I remember thinking that we had to settle down a little. Pull back on the drugs and the lifestyle. It was wearing us both down and I was suffering from migraines that were just awful.

But, that sort of change just doesn't take place overnight.

We moved into a unit in Burwood and that was when we got engaged. It's important at this time to mention something I said to David.

You know we all have those significant moments in our lives that are burned in our memory?

This was one of mine.

David always tried to communicate with me via poems. He would write pages of words and give them to me. The trouble was I was so shut down inside that the words had no meaning at all. I just couldn't understand them.

My Return To Love

I didn't even know just how shut down I was.

When we spoke about spending the rest of our lives together, I declared to him, *"I just want you to know that my emotional extent is good, bad, happy, sad. Don't expect anything more from me."*

He was okay with that. What a crazy declaration to make.

I was essentially saying, don't expect any depth from me because it was impossible.

We then moved to Blackburn. I started work with the law firm, *Perry Weston*, and David started working and training as a manager with a major department store. With each move we got a little cleaner, a little clearer, a little more off the drugs.

I encouraged it; it was needed. David's access to his son was a blessing; it required discipline and responsibility.

You couldn't settle down and have a family if there were drugs around, right? That was my reasoning; I never stopped to consider what David's thinking was.

I never stopped to consider that drugs could possibly have been the reason for the breakdown of his first marriage…

MARRIED

On the 23rd May 1987, we got married. It was the same church that Scott and Charlene got married in. Remember the TV series *Neighbours* with Kylie Minogue and Jason Donovan?

It was a beautiful bluestone church in Doncaster East, and we followed with a reception at Arleigh in Malvern. Arleigh was owned by my friend Jeanette's parents and had a fabulous history of being a regular hangout for Squizzy Taylor. He was a famous gangster in the late 1800s.

The venue had secret doors and even tunnels that went from Malvern all the way underground to the centre of Melbourne. My dad was affectionately nicknamed 'Squizzy' by his friends; I think because he could be just as notorious as the original 'Squizzy Taylor'.

It seemed a fitting place for us to have our reception.

Stopping drugs meant moving away from people doing drugs. I could stop, I had many good reasons to. David struggled a little more. He was the one that needed to lose a few more friends than me. There was no more speed in our lives and no more dope.

It was time to settle down and be a 'normal' couple and prepare to have a family.

I know David struggled through this time. How did I know?

Well, whenever we went out, I always had to drive home because David would get drunk. Sometimes, he would pass out. It wasn't all the time, but it was enough times to tell me that he had a problem.

At my sister's 21st birthday party, David left early. I got home to find that the large glass sliding door to the side of the house had been smashed in. David did it.

He got home earlier without a key and that was his solution for getting into the house and crashing out in bed. I was about six months pregnant at the time and it totally freaked me out.

Cameron was born in July 1988, followed by our twin boys Shane and Gavin in August 1990. We both loved being parents. I was a stay-at-home mum and ran the house and the routine with the kids like clockwork. Raising three small kids was certainly a full-time job.

David was moving up the ranks at work. He was working at a level he had never had before, and it came with a lot of responsibility and pressure.

It was at this time that a few cracks started to appear in our relationship. A few of his friends started to creep back onto the scene. It started by them just hanging out in the garage playing table tennis, then having a few joints and a few beers.

His behaviour started to change, and I knew, a woman always knows, that there was flirting or something more going on at his work. There were signs.

I knew I needed to address these things, but I just didn't know how. I suppose I just didn't know what would happen if I did. I was scared to face them, so I just focused on everything else.

But what happens to the things you don't face? They grow.

We outgrew the house and upgraded to another home which happened to be only a few blocks away. It had a great big backyard which was perfect for three growing boys. It was walking distance from school, kindergarten, the playgrounds, shops which was great for me because we only had one car which, of course, David needed to get to and from work.

Overall, life was pretty good for all of us.

HERE COME THE CRACKS

I'm not sure exactly what the trigger or turning point was. The cracks just got bigger and bigger and the gap between us got larger. Both of us were feeling all sorts of stuff that was pretty uncomfortable.

David wrote about it in poems, trying to connect with me – while I was so shut down by now that I couldn't even understand the words on the paper.

David's old friends and even my old friend Linda began to creep back into our lives. Smoking dope became more popular and more regular, then the speed came back in. It was becoming a mess again and, this time, we had three kids.

We convinced ourselves that everything was okay. I would again have to be the driver whenever we went out because David would drink himself stupid. He was even starting to have black outs when I couldn't even wake him to get out of the car when we arrived home. I would carry three kids into their beds and leave him out in the car.

Red flag.

Underneath it all, I knew he was being unfaithful, and it certainly turned me away from wanting any closeness with him. I started to see him differently. I started to see all the things that were wrong. The drugs were good because they just filled the big black hole that was growing in our lives.

And then along came the craziest curve ball ever. You see David, probably through my brother, had found someone else to buy drugs through. His name was Andrew. I actually went to school with him, he was a few years above me.

I knew of him but didn't actually know him. We needed to score some speed, so David rang him, and Andrew came around to our house to deliver.

When you are doing speed, you do all sorts of things at the strangest hours. It was 9pm at night, kids were in bed, and David and I were painting the family room. Andrew came around and, as soon as I met him, something happened.

I have no words for it, it was a certain kind of energy. We connected in some strange way that just wouldn't make sense for me until much later.

During his visit, I found out that he owned the local brothel and had to go quickly because something was going on and he had to perform security duties for the girls. I was very curious about all that and, we all know by now what curiosity does for me.

As he left, he made a quick comment to me, *"We need a receptionist, let me know if you want a job."*

After he left, David suggested I follow it up.

I was totally bewildered. Why would he even suggest it?

He argued, why not, any extra money would be good and if it was at night time, he would be around to look after the kids.

WHAT COMES FROM CURIOSITY?

Curiosity had me.

I had never been in a brothel, so I made an appointment for an interview with Andrew's business partner who would take me on a tour of the place. I don't know how to describe my visit.

From the moment I walked into the place, everything felt so surreal. There was a reception area, a side room where the girls relaxed and waited for bookings and then four different rooms set up with beds, spas and low lighting. I got so disorientated I couldn't remember how to make my way back to the front door.

It was incredible.

They had two shifts available, a Tuesday night and a Sunday daytime. I took the job.

These are a few things I learned really fast:

- I was incredibly naive.
- The mattresses in the rooms only had a fitted sheet over them. They didn't need blankets or doonas, of course.
- You will get hit on many times, propositioned; and must learn how to handle it.
- Telling men I was married didn't work.
- Everyone was 'the receptionist'. I soon discovered that all the working girls told people they were the receptionist.

My Return To Love

- You get prank phone calls or dirty phone calls and must learn how to handle them.
- The girls are all paranoid and will blame you for anything they can.
- It's a real dog-eat-dog world; one I had never experienced before.

I loved it though.

My job involved answering the front door, showing the client into a room, having the girls' parade through one at a time, going back to see who has been chosen, make the booking, take the payment and letting the girl do her thing.

I would knock on the door when there was five minutes to go, letting them know that 'time was up' and that was about it for me.

I had to handle any disputes that may take place in the room or even in the girls' room. It certainly tested me, but I have always been pretty good at thinking on my feet.

How did I get to this place in life?

Married, three kids, running part time conveyancing from home during the day, secretary of the local multiple birth club group which involved supporting local parents, attending meetings, two days a week at a brothel… All while still doing drugs and running on pure adrenaline.

No wonder I started to have panic attacks.

The first one happened when I was driving to the supermarket. I didn't have a car during the day so Mum would come around, usually while the kids were having a nap – that's how I planned it – and I would go to the supermarket.

In my mind, I would have limited time. I didn't want Mum having to handle all the kids while they were awake, so I would rush to supermarket, get groceries and get back home.

I left the house, drove up the street, got to the end of the street and had no idea whether to turn right or left and absolutely no idea where I was actually going.

Panic set in.

I had at least the sense to stop, breathe and wait to get some insight.

It was awful; panic attacks are awful.

Larger cracks were appearing between me and David. We needed more drugs to keep going. I found new confidence working in the brothel and a new friend in Tracey. She was pretty grounded compared to a lot of the women. She had a young son and was doing her best to provide for them.

Occasionally, I would go out with her to a local nightclub. I needed the dance floor; I desperately needed to offload the stress and worry somehow.

FATAL ATTRACTION

There was also another problem at this time. It was about me and Andrew. I would see him at the brothel – sometimes when he delivered drugs to our home and, from time to time, he would drive me home after my night shift. It saved me a taxi and he lived only a few minutes from our place.

The problem was there was a tremendous amount of energy happening between us. It was electric and it was something I had never experienced before.

I felt it every time I saw him, and it increased whenever we were alone together in the car. It was strong and incredibly attractive, but I would not act on it. I was married and, for me personally, it was important never to cheat on someone I was in a relationship with.

A lot of this time of my life is still a blur to me. Drugs probably had a lot to do with that.

Ultimately though, I knew my marriage was over.

We weren't communicating. I couldn't communicate, the gap between us felt overwhelming and, for me, it was turning into anger and resentment and that wasn't good.

There came a time when I knew David and I were done; I just had to have the courage to tell him. That wasn't so easy though, because there was also a lot of fear in the way. I spoke to no one about the situation; I had no-one I could trust to confide in.

I had no idea how I was going to manage if we split up, but it had to be done; all the ideas or solutions I came up with all ended up a disaster, but I knew it couldn't go on like this.

That's when the incident happened; the one I spoke about right at the beginning of this book.

The voice that told me to get out.

It knew the marriage had to end and it was the catalyst for me taking one of the biggest steps in my life.

So, I slept with Andrew. I knew by taking this step that I was declaring the end to my marriage. This was my way of forcing myself to ruin it, to finish it.

Little did I realise, but I also gave David a great excuse to not want to be with me anymore.

Andrew and I were drawn together like magnets, and it ignited something deep within me; a love for him that was overwhelming.

I had to be with him, I had to connect with him. He was on my mind morning, noon and night. He consumed me. Little did I know at the time, but I had triggered something known as karma.

Karma has no rhyme or reason to it for the ignorant and uninitiated like me. It was something I would find out more about in the not-too-distant future.

MY MARRIAGE WAS OVER

Soon after, I told David we were over. I wanted to separate. At first, I thought we could do it living under the same roof. Such an idealist I was – it was never going to work.

David was angry and I also began to find out just how much he had been undermining me to my friends and family. I had no idea that he had been planting seeds with them all; painting me out to be the problem, implying that I was 'losing it'.

He had to leave; it was getting ugly.

As the idealist, I have always aimed to find the best solution to any situation, to see the best in people and I thought that all people would act reasonably – no matter what was going on.

That's how I would act. I really thought that everybody thought things through like I did. How incredibly naive, hey?

David left and not long after, Tracey and her son moved in with us. It was a win/win for both of us. It certainly helped me with the bills.

Chapter 6

THE GAME CHANGER

ANDREW

I was 33 years old. I started seeing Andrew on a regular basis and decided to move on from working at his brothel; it was becoming increasingly uneasy as the working girls discovered I was seeing Andrew.

In that world, there was a lot of small mindedness among some.

Tracey was mainly working at *Masquerades*, and she got me an interview with the bosses. They ran a well-oiled machine; a much bigger establishment than Andrew had. They had a bar, pool tables and games areas for entertainment and they also had computer systems for bookings and payments.

I got the job, and they trained me for a week on the systems before I could actually work in the brothel itself.

This was a whole other level.

It wasn't my job to see the clients into a room. They had a hostess who took care of that for every shift. It was her job to rev up the customers and get them booking the girls.

I just had to monitor room bookings and payments – as well as monitor behaviour and the surrounding carparks because if there was any sign of trouble, I had to call security.

One thing that was very important though; it was paramount that the girls liked me because they chose which shifts they wanted to work and that certainly depended on who the receptionist was as well.

Tracey put the word out about me, which was very helpful.

The biggest problem for me; I was still doing the drugs. Andrew just also happened to be a drug dealer and he would come across some of the purest and best stuff to be had.

As his girlfriend, I got my fair share of it. It was highly addictive.

There was another problem with being Andrew's girlfriend. He began asking to borrow money from me. He was always doing deals and that included money. One minute, he had stacks of it and next minute, he was scrambling for it.

Borrowing from me started to increase and I readily helped out, always thinking I was going to get it back soon. I had no idea I was never going to get it back.

When I would ask for some or all of it; it created hostility and arguments. I'd never come across this before and really didn't know how to handle it.

My income was the single parent pension and earning money from a couple of shifts at *Masquerades* per week and, because Andrew was regularly getting money from me, I had to make more money somehow. I was getting so desperate.

I started dealing the speed for him and started keeping a tiny notebook with details of the dates and amounts he was getting from me. I had to keep record.

It was like an alternate universe.

I had never lived in a world where people lied, cheated, stole and manipulated to get whatever they wanted and to sort things out; this was done by shouting, yelling, aggressive tactics.

It was a dog-eat-dog world and survival of the fittest, cunning and craftiest. But ironically, this is where I found myself.

I was totally disillusioned and out of my depth. I didn't know how to operate like this but, what I did know, I had better adapt and do it quick in order to survive.

Survival mode is chaos.

Tracey could see the writing on the wall for me. She didn't do the drugs and could see what Andrew was doing to me. She moved out.

I had to step it up and earn even more money. I was running on empty.

DISOWNED

My father had told all the family to have nothing to do with me.

My in-laws had been told by David to have nothing to do with me and, David, was not paying anything towards the kids. Desperation was creeping in all around me.

I cried myself to sleep a lot. My brain was fried; I just couldn't think straight so I was living moment to moment just trying to manage things; terrified that at any moment I wouldn't have enough money, wouldn't have a place to live.

I was behind on rent, behind with bills and Andrew would just shut me down when I asked for some money back.

Me and the kids were evicted. The sheriff came, changed the locks and threw us out. We had nowhere to go.

We slept in the car the first night and then *Wesley Mission* put us up in a motel. I had hit rock bottom; so, I thought.

I had to find somewhere for us to live and I was so angry because Andrew owed me so much money, money that would completely change my situation. Money that had caused my current situation and I just couldn't get it back off him.

Somehow, someway I found the courage to demand Andrew help us. He reluctantly agreed that we move into his place. Three kids and all their belongings in one bedroom. A bunch of men smoking bongs in the lounge room, people coming and going at all hours; it was hardly paradise.

We all settled in and made the best of a crazy situation. Andrew came and went as he pleased. We had no relationship at all. He slept during the day, and I slept, during the night. I began to realise that his version of a relationship was something more like ownership.

For him, it was best that he did whatever he wanted and I just 'fitted in' when required. I started to see the cracks appearing between us and I started to hear the stories about other women, to hear excuses about where he was and what he was doing. He didn't like having to be accountable for anything and would get really angry.

I just wanted to keep him happy because the anger was scary so I just focused on the kids and getting them to school and kindergarten, focused on selling as much of the drugs as I could to make as much money for him as I could. I was becoming another person altogether.

I had trouble getting to sleep and I had trouble waking up in the mornings. I spent my time alone during the school hours going to the laundromat, doing housework, listening to music and crying.

I did a lot of crying. I felt so totally alone.

I had no-one to turn to. No-one to talk things out with. I had never felt so alone in my entire life.

Deep down, I knew I had gone off the rails and that I couldn't keep living like this, but I just didn't know what to do; I just couldn't see a way out, so I just kept going, day by day, over and over doing the same things and day dreaming for a solution.

THE NERVOUS BREAKDOWN

It was here that I had my nervous breakdown. One evening after the kids were settled to sleep, I went outside to take a walk. I was feeling so lost and alone and I just needed to get some fresh air.

It was summer and it was still pretty warm outside. I had a light skirt and t-shirt on and no shoes on. I remember going around to the side of the house and looking into the lounge room window. Inside, was Andrew and a few friends all laughing and talking. That made me feel even worse.

What had happened to me?

Only a few months ago, I had been married with a husband, kids, family, security, support and now it was all gone… Everything.

I felt so defeated and I started to cry.

That night I walked the streets looking into the windows of homes, seeing families enjoying comfort, security, laughter, company. I was totally broken; I couldn't stop crying.

From time to time, I would collapse in the gardens of other peoples' homes, sobbing and full of despair. I was totally losing it; out of control, breaking down completely.

Eventually, I made my way back to Andrew's and went to bed.

I woke up the next morning a different person.

You see I'd actually had a nervous breakdown the night before. I didn't know that at the time, but I had. I think it was probably

10 years overdue, but I had finally surrendered and allowed it to happen.

I woke to find that I had a lot of energy and I had a totally new focus. I felt renewed and determined to find solutions for my current problems.

Uppermost on my mind was finding a job, finding a new place to live and start rebuilding my life for myself and especially for my kids.

I felt strong for the first time in a long time.

And then a little miracle happened; my nan gave us some money. God bless her.

It came via my Auntie because my mum still wasn't allowed to see me. That money paid for a caravan for us in a local caravan park. I don't remember much of this time except that Andrew often came to visit, mostly for sex, drugs or money, and one of the neighbours was a lovely older woman.

Immediately, she befriended us and seemed to look out for us; she was a caring mother figure and made me feel safe.

The money for the caravan park was about to run out and along came my brother, another miracle, with a solution. He recommended us for a house that he and his wife had just vacated. It was a wonderful gesture on his part but unfortunately, I wasn't a very good option.

The kids and I moved into a new home ourselves and I got myself a part time job; another miracle.

My Auntie offered it to me. Again, it was another good gesture but unfortunately, I wasn't ready for it, I couldn't make that consistent commitment – not for long anyway.

You see I had sunk so low and, because of the drug use and abusive relationship I was in, I was behaving like all the 'strugglers' around me.

Do you hear what I'm saying here?

When you live in the dog-eat-dog world of drugs, prostitution and moral decay; you constantly operate in survival. Survival includes lying, cheating, backstabbing, no conscious, no ethics.

I was so naïve, so innocent to the depraved ways that these people thought and acted.

Since that first time I walked into Andrew's brothel, I had witnessed many pretty disgusting things and was hanging around the outskirts of some pretty dangerous people, too. Many people and situations I came across scared me.

I knew I had to get back to some semblance of who I was. At least I had a reference point of what I wanted to get back to. I knew what it was like to live a comfortable life, with a job, regular money and family and friends. I wanted it all back.

It was going to be a difficult road, but I had to do it. I knew it wasn't going to be easy but, what I didn't realise was, that this lower way of life was going to try to stop me from leaving… But it was.

My problem was still the drugs.

The Game Changer

When you're doing drugs regularly, you're constantly in a state of fight and flight. You're constantly in survival mode. Add to that the people and the world I was living in and that just multiplies the fear factor by a 100.

Even though some family were stepping back into my life and offering a helping hand; none of them knew the extent that drugs had a hold of me and, even if they did, none of them knew what to do to help.

I couldn't keep down the part-time job and I still couldn't keep enough money from Andrew so I could pay rent.

I was about to be evicted again so I dug down deeper into myself and started to plan the next move. I knew something had to change or else.

I got another house because by now I had learnt how to lie and cheat enough to get myself a lease. I had to be prepared to do anything to look after my kids now.

It was perfect, just down the road from where all three children were now going to school. The kids and I moved in, and Andrew moved in shortly after. Yes, he moved in, too.

Andrew claimed his house was being taken over by the other people he had let stay and he wanted to move out; he wanted to get away from them all. Well, that's the story he told me.

I found out years later that the real reason was much more sinister than that.

Stupid me, still so scared of him that I couldn't say no. Stupid me for being so naive to think that I could still make us work. Stupid me for being so addicted to drugs that I couldn't let him go.

Stupid me indeed.

GLIMPSES OF REALITY

It was about this time that I started to realise that Andrew and I had two very different ideas about how life and relationships went. I settled into being the mother and partner. I knew those roles very well. I ran the house, cooked, cleaned, got the kids to and from school, ate meals together, had baths, showers and went to bed. That meant going to bed at night-time with my partner, Andrew.

That never happened.

He never ate with us, never did family things with us and never came to bed at night and slept with me.

The house had a back family room that had been partly built on. The walls and external were finished but the internal had not been completed at all. It needed plaster sheets, cornices and window finishes etc.

Andrew wanted to do the work. I asked the landlords, and they were happy to have it done as long as they didn't have to pay.

To get to that back room, you had to leave through the back door of the house, down a few stairs and the door to the family room was on your right. That meant that you could come and go from that room without going into the main house at all.

Andrew got all the work done and it became his part of the house. He only came into the main house for a shower and to say goodnight to the kids.

I was devastated.

This was not what I wanted but what could I do?

Andrew avoided any conversations with me about us and, to be honest, I tiptoed around them because I was afraid of how violent he would become.

Then the good speed arrived. It was the ultimate pure speed that you could possibly get. I felt superhuman on it.

We got to have the pure stuff and cut the rest of it down to sell to others.

For a little while, life was wonderful, lots of good speed and lots of good money to be made.

I was, however, more concerned about Andrew's behaviour. *Hells Angel* members were coming round to the house. I was walking in on conversations about guns, dynamite and other unthinkable stuff. I didn't like any of this at all, but I was riding the high from this latest speed and pushed aside my concerns for a while.

Of course, this ride was going to end.

Like all things with drugs, they run in cycles and the good relationship Andrew had with the man supplying the drugs started to go south. Suspicion, bad behaviour and money issues started to creep in.

The guy did not like the 'bikies' getting involved and he walked away.

Andrew had been getting just as fried as me with this new level of speed and, when the supplied disappeared, he crashed and crashed hard.

Anything would spark him; he had a short fuse but now it had gotten much shorter. I began to tiptoe around him, terrified of setting him off.

Our only conversations now were about money, he needed more and more. It had to stop, I could not let this go on anymore, but I was so scared, and fear had me completely paralysed. I was overthinking all my options but was afraid to do anything at all.

I remember one day thinking about what was going on when I had this thought:

"How was I, a well-educated, strong, middle-class women, stuck in this horrible relationship? How did I get to this point in my life? How is this even possible?"

And then, the next realisation I had…

I had become my mum. I had often judged my mum during my life. I watched how Dad had treated her. He used to cut off the money supply, so she couldn't buy groceries. He used to take the telephone to work with him, so she couldn't use it. He played mind games with her and was abusive.

I remember thinking there was no way that I would ever put up with being treated that way and that I would leave. I certainly wouldn't stay 'for the kids'. I thought she was 'weak' for staying with him.

What a realisation.

Had I become my mum? I was horrified.

Something happened after my realisation. Cracks appeared and I began to see things more clearly.

KNOCK, KNOCK, KNOCKING ON DEATH'S DOOR

By now, Andrew owed me over AUD$4,000 – yes, I still had my little notebook, our relationship was nothing more than accommodation and yes, he was sleeping with other women, many of them.

The tipping point: I weighed myself. I weighed 50kg because of the drugs and the constant stress, and I knew I was going to die if something didn't change.

My anger started to come out.

I started to undermine him; I started to get critical; I started to stand my ground until all hell broke loose.

A bunch of people had just left the back room – the one Andrew lived in most of the time. They had been buying drugs. I went down to the room for some reason, I can't recall.

Immediately, I could tell that Andrew was angry. Something was very, very wrong.

My Return To Love

All it took was a few words out of my mouth and he flew at me. His face was vicious and full of rage. He put his hands around my throat; all the time screaming at me and picked me right up off the floor. I knew that I had just taken my last breath.

There was no way I could speak, there was no way I could fight him off; he was much too strong for me, and I knew I was about to die.

There was absolutely nothing I could do.

I remember distinctly thinking to myself, *"If he lets me go, I will do whatever it takes."*

It was such a clear and precise thought right in the middle of such horror and crises. And, at that exact moment, he let me go and stormed out of the room.

I know something heard me that day. I know something knew that I would do whatever it took to get me and my children out of that situation.

It was time.

I have no idea what heard me, but I *know* something did.

I woke up the next morning and began the job of reclaiming my life piece by piece.

Incredibly, it took nearly dying as the catalyst.

Overnight, I stopped drugs.

Truly overnight. No more speed, no more marijuana, nothing, I just stopped.

Mind you, Andrew kept giving me daily doses of drugs like usual and I started stashing them away in a drawer.

I also began stashing away money. Bit by bit, money also went away into another drawer.

Next, I started looking through the newspapers for a job. I started submitting applications, making telephone calls and finally got accepted for a sales position. It involved going to Queensland for training.

I went without hesitation.

I could really feel the doors to my old self opening up again. My mind was clearer and, funnily enough, I had no withdrawals. I think I kept waiting to have them because everyone says you do.

It just didn't happen at all.

It was at this time that my world turned into a whirlwind of possibilities. Everything began to change.

CHANGING FOR THE BETTER

Mum started to make contact with us. She was a brave woman. Secretly sometimes, she would walk all the way to our house just so no one else would know. She loved me and her grandsons and struggled a lot without seeing us.

It was a welcome sight to see her occasionally; better than not at all.

Also, Jane came into my life. She came around from time to time to score from Andrew but we immediately hit it off.

She was a mystical woman. She knew a lot about how life worked. Her parents were Rosicrucian and had raised her through that faith.

I remember clearly what she said to me, *"I hope I'm not in your life for six months and then I'm gone."*

Because she was…

We spent many hours talking all things spiritual. I knew nothing at all about any of this stuff and was so intrigued about astrology, meditation, telepathy, energy and spirits. She was like a breath of fresh air.

Little by little, I gained more energy and more vitality for life. It still wasn't easy. I had a long way to go. I still had to negotiate Andrew. Even though I was stashing money away; he still did his best to get his hands on whatever I had, and I still didn't have enough confidence to do anything about it.

You know he had done a really good job in convincing me that any bad behaviour by him was caused by me. Slowly but surely, he had me believing that it was always the way I acted, the things I said that made him behave badly.

It's crazy but true how someone can do that to you. So, I still gave him money, just not as much.

Then, another miracle came along.

I remember at one point having no money for food. Nothing at all and I just couldn't figure out how I was going to feed the kids until the next pension payment. I did a lot of crying one morning, but I knew that crying doesn't make money.

So, I got stuck into cleaning the house.

I was at the kitchen sink doing the dishes when a voice loud and clear in my head said, *"Open the door."*

Memories of the voice telling me to 'get out' certainly crossed my mind, but this was different. This voice was in my head. It was clear and insistent, and I knew it wasn't me.

Once again, not being able to explain it, I got back to doing the dishes. But once again, there it was, a voice in my head that said, *"Open the door."*

I was terrified and curious all at the same time. I knew the only thing I could do was go to the front door and open it. I did.

As soon as I opened the door, Jane pushed passed me with groceries bags in her hands. She said, *"What took you so long?! You know your doorbell doesn't work, don't you?"*

I was overwhelmed.

Firstly, she had brought me groceries. She knew what Andrew was doing to me and she knew how much I was struggling.

She told me not to worry, it only cost her AUD$60 and she was more than happy to do it. Then, she explained the telepathy.

She had been taught that through the Rosicrucian Order. She said it was easy to do and she would begin to teach me about energy and many other things.

WHAT WAS THIS THING CALLED SPIRITUALITY?

My spiritual world opened up.

Jane gave me an astrology deck of cards with instructions on how to do readings. I also bought myself a tarot deck at an op shop together with a book of instructions for it as well. She began to teach me about mediation and energy and, of course, telepathy. I was very curious about it and so eager to learn.

I remember that I had a new like for crosses. I brought myself a few, just costume jewellery, and I began to wear them but no matter what, they would fall off. It was hard to figure out.

If I wore a chain, the chain would break and the cross would fall of. So, I tried a thin leather strap, tied a knot in it and hung that around my neck and, guess what, the cross fell off.

Welcome to the world of the unknown and unseen.

This new learning started to fill me up from the inside out and it brough such joy into my life. I started to really pull away from Andrew and needed less and less of a connection with him.

I even remember times when Andrew and his friends would have a shortage of their drug supply; I would give him what I had stashed away.

He never questioned it; that's how stupid greed is.

I got cleverer with money and made sure I had very little in my purse. So, whenever he asked me for money; I would open up my purse, make excuses for where the rest had gone, and he slowly stopped asking me anymore.

Nearly dying at the hands of Andrew was a blessing in disguise.

Since that event, my life took a 180º turn for the better and, piece by piece, new things started to open up for me.

Next, I came across an advert in the local paper. It was for a healing session with an energy healer.

> *INSIGHT: I had lived in the eastern suburbs all my life. There were three particular local groups of shops that I had been to many times. So how had I never noticed that there was a new age shop or crystal shop in each of those places? Now, as I turned my mind to all things spiritual; I could see these shops when in the past I must have walked right passed them. What did that mean?*

I rang her to make an appointment for a healing and booked myself in. I had no idea what to expect but went with an open mind.

She lived not far from me and invited me into a very comfortable room. It was all set up with a massage table covered in blankets and beautiful surroundings including crystals, incense and many things to look at.

Her name was Sylvanna and she sat me down to explain a little of what would happen during a session. She said that she worked with energy and that at various times in our life, our energy would become blocked which could cause mental, emotional or physical problems.

The whole thing happened with me fully dressed, lying on the comfortable massage bed and with some peaceful, calming music playing. I didn't have to do anything. I was happy about that.

I couldn't explain anything that happened to me that day. All I knew was when I left her; I felt lighter, calmer and all the thoughts in my head had stopped. The world just seemed a better place than it had before.

She explained that I had several blocks in my lower chakras; she explained a little about the chakra system, told me she had, with the help of her spirit guides, removed the blocks and my energy was now moving freely. She highly recommended another session, so I booked myself in again.

I loved this experience; I loved what she was capable of doing and it all went hand in hand with my astrology and tarot studies I had been doing.

I had started giving tarot readings and found I was extremely good at them. I had a gift for reading the cards and for reading a person's energy field and I just loved doing them.

The combination of Jane's friendship, my growing stash of money and my healing sessions with Sylvanna led to the next step.

It was time to finish things with Andrew and move on.

Andrew had made it pretty clear that there was no way he was going to let go of me so, with my newfound support network, I went to the police and applied for an intervention order.

Andrew was served and, at that same time, I found a new house to move into and moved me and the kids out.

I was free.

It felt so liberating and incredibly scary all at the same time. Andrew wasn't allowed to call me or visit me, and, with the help of Sylvanna, who had now become a constant friend, I felt safe and began to build a new life for myself and the kids.

It was a beautiful house and with it, came a lot of changes. David started to have more connection with the kids, my mum and sister Dianne started to come and visit.

The door to my family was beginning to open up again.

My healing sessions with Sylvanna had turned into long conversations with her. She was building a business. She wanted to help anyone in the healing industry to grow their business and she wanted me to help. She needed to hand over some of the healing work to someone else so she could focus more on the growth of the healing management business. She asked if I wanted to do it.

I was over the moon. Of course, I would; I just loved having healing sessions and now she would teach and guide me into giving healing sessions, as well.

I continued with my personal healing sessions which also turned into learning meditation and the importance of journaling. My sessions were bringing up many childhood memories for me to face; issues with my parents and I began to tackle them one at a time.

I began to have memories of events that had never happened in this life and Sylvanna explained to me about past lives. She was pretty sure that my relationship with Andrew had been one in a past life.

She encouraged me to write and release things and suggested I study the Native Americans, especially the behaviour of the wolf because this would teach me a lot about opening my heart and living life that way.

I read every book, watched every movie and learned a lot about energy, spirit guides, the chakra system, crystals and the heart.

During this time, strange things began to happen in the house we were living in. Lights would flicker on and off, the television screen, and even the radio, wouldn't work properly from time to time. Sometimes, there would be the smell of smoke and something began tapping in one of the walls in the kitchen behind a clock that I had on the wall.

Sylvanna came around to investigate.

It seemed two things were going on. Andrew was angry and projecting his energy into the house. Also, there was a spirit in the house, his name was Tommy, and he didn't really like any of us living there.

I was about to learn about energetic protection.

The Game Changer

Protection of myself, my children and the house. With Sylvanna, we performed a ceremony, smudged the house, created a circle of protection and the energy changed.

But it wasn't over yet.

Chapter 7

PAST LIVES, SPIRIT GUIDES AND DEMONS

I call this next phase of my life, *'the quickening'*, because it's the only way to explain an escalated period of learning. I learnt a lot and I learnt it fast.

However, it wasn't like learning; it was like remembering.

Childhood memories were coming up, I was studying spirituality, working as a healer, studying past lives, learning about spirit guides and demons, navigating David and my family coming back into our lives, and navigating Andrew trying to reconnect.

How did he find me?

He rung the telephone at the house and left a message. How did he get my number?

Instincts told me it was David. You know it wasn't the first time David had thrown me under the bus. He had given out my details, I was sure of it.

The personal work I did on myself was opening up other dimensions of myself and other dimensions of this world. I was more clairvoyant, more psychic, more intuitive and much more aware of the energy of the people around me and was starting to see spirits – whatever you want to call them.

I crossed the line… Andrew rang, and I answered the phone. He wanted to come around and I let him.

I know. What was I thinking? What was I doing?

You know I could do anything with him when he wasn't around. I could talk about what I was going to say, what I was going to do but, when his energy met with mine, something else happened.

I couldn't explain what it was. Call it karma, call it my insecurities, call it unfinished business; I just don't know what it was but, when we connected, I just couldn't control myself.

As a result, I broke the intervention order.

When he came round, he was really different. He behaved himself, treated me well. He offered me some marijuana, a peace offering, so we smoked some together and slept together.

I broke every new rule I had set for myself; all in one night.

I remember catching myself thinking, *"Oh this is great, he's finally changed. He's finally acting like I always wanted him to."*

For a moment, I had the feeling that something wasn't quite right.

I had many other times in my life when someone told me that they had changed or that they could change. Dad said he could change, Greg said he could change, David said he could change, Linda said she could change.

None of them did. I had never seen anyone actually follow through with the changes. They were always short lived.

SPIRITUAL GROWTH AND HEALING

My son Shane sleepwalked from time to time and I woke one night to find him going through the drawer of the tall boy in his room. I proceeded gently and asked him what he was doing. He said Tommy wanted him to find a lighter.

He wanted it so Shane could burn the house down.

I steered Shane from his bedroom into the bathroom down the hall. I figured I would get a warm face cloth and wash his face so he could slowly wake up. I ran the tap and moistened the face cloth.

When I turned back to Shane, I was shocked to find that his face was overlaid by the face of a green demon-looking thing. His skin was green, his ears were pointed, and his face was a different shape.

I immediately and firmly told the thing that it had no right to have anything to do with my son and demanded that it leave right away. It did!

Shane woke up and was totally bewildered. I calmly told him he had been sleepwalking and washed his face. He thought he had been dreaming and told me he knew Tommy was there and he was getting to him to find a lighter.

I told him I had sent him away. He slept with me the rest of that night.

At this time, Steve had just come into my life. He was a good friend of Sylvanna and was touted as a psychic and esoteric teacher. He had his own modality called *'The 'Method'* a healing system that he taught to hundreds of students.

I was so intrigued by him.

He could read your mind and read your energy and knew so much stuff about spirituality. I was in awe of him.

We spent a lot of time together. We went for walks, trips to the country, picnics, the movies and I really enjoyed his company. He was forever teaching me things and I took it all on board.

Never for a second did I think that this was becoming a relationship. I suppose I was pretty starstruck and saw him as a guru. He was a musician as well and even wrote a song for me called 'Helen's Song'.

I still didn't catch on. I still had the capacity to be incredibly naive.

He was about to become part of a very big experience I was to have. It was about the harm that can be done when casting spells.

My childhood stuff was really emerging, I was recalling two particular nightmares I used to have as a child: I would be walking home from school, just at the bottom of our street, and a big dog would come and grab me and throw me down the drain and, the other dream, a big black dog would grab me, take me to the Botanical Gardens (which were a part of Melbourne City) and throw me right over a very high wire fence. That fence was the high impenetrable security fence that surrounded a very big mansion. Elton John was inside that mansion, and I was terrified of having to go inside.

This all lead to me recalling the abuse that had taken place when I was a child; I started to remember it all.

I experienced the whole gamut of emotions as these memories came flooding back and I swung between confronting my dad and not confronting him.

I worked with Sylvanna, talking through things, writing a lot, healing sessions and meditations. My conclusion: this was something I needed to process myself. Confronting Dad, telling Mum, anything else would just cause such pain.

I couldn't do that. One thing that did concern me though; did my sisters suffer the same abuse?

Leonie had difficulty being around me. We were on such different wave lengths and just couldn't communicate. With Dianne, I needed to speak to her when the time was right.

That opportunity arose not long after. She came around to visit. I picked the time and began to tell her that I had started to remember something that happened to me as a child.

What happened next was extraordinary.

She couldn't hear me. She said she had a loud buzzing in her ears which was so loud she couldn't hear me. She said that she was feeling weird, and her head was spinning. She was so distressed and couldn't understand what was happening to her.

I stopped and, as soon as I did, she began to feel better. She kept repeating, *"What just happened? What just happened?!"*

I told her I didn't know but I was glad she was feeling better.

I had just witnessed one of the most amazing physiological reactions by someone who, clearly, did NOT want to hear what I was about to say. How do you explain that?

My reconnection with Mum grew stronger and stronger and finally I felt comfortable enough to go around to their home and met with Dad.

Just like all throughout my life, I walked back in as though nothing had ever happened.

There were no apologies, no discussion about what had gone on; no recognition of the trouble I had been through. Nothing, zippo. So typical of my family.

Everything was always left as unfinished businesses. Nothing ever got fully resolved.

Oh well, I was back, and I was actually very happy to be able to visit them once again and especially happy that my boys could now also come back around. They missed their Nanna and Pa.

I think subconsciously I really wanted to hold Dad to account. I found myself challenging him in conversations whenever I could, pushing and prying a little further. I really wanted to know what made him 'tick'. With my newfound way of looking at things, I discovered I really didn't know him very well at all.

Sometimes, we got a little deeper into conversations about his health, which included the bowel cancer and, into the future, panic attacks and emphysema. He was also beginning to suffer from phantom pain in his missing arm.

This wasn't the first time that sort of pain arose. I had no idea that he had tried various alternative therapies many years back to help with the same thing. We had more in common than I thought.

I was now offering massage as well as the healing sessions through the business with Sylvanna. Dad found out about this, and I would occasionally give him a massage to alleviate the pain and discomfort in his arm, shoulders and back.

Who would have thought? I welcomed this new connection with him.

REUNITING WITH FAMILY

These renewed connections with the family were wonderful, but not without problems. I remember one occasion when we were gathered at Mum and Dad's for a lunch get together. Mum, Dad, my sisters Leonie and Dianne, my brother Mark and his wife, Rhonda.

Rhonda was a bit rough around the edges. I'm just being honest. I really liked her but sometimes, when she had a few too many drinks, she would get brassier and louder. This was one of those times. I think I just mentally took note of that for some reason.

We were all in the open plan kitchen/family room and I remember that I was talking. I was pretty happy about the spiritual path I was walking down, and I think I was saying something about how liberating it was and how I had less anger now. Next thing, Rhonda runs around the kitchen bench and straight at me. She launched herself through the air and was about to punch me right in the face.

My brother, from somewhere to the right of me, leapt in, grabbed Rhonda just before she connected her fist with my face and took her kicking and screaming down the hallway and out the front door of the house.

My dad was standing across from me. He glared at me and turned to take after Mark out the front door.

I looked to my left and Mum was crying. She left out the back door to go into the garden. My sisters followed her.

I was left all alone in the house.

I was in shock. What had just happened? I had no idea, so I did a quick review.

One minute, I was standing in the kitchen talking. Everyone seemed okay. Rhonda was agitated and seemed to have had a few too many drinks but what the hell did I do that made her want to try to punch me in the face? I didn't know.

What to do next?

I certainly wasn't going to follow my brother. I did not want to deal with Rhonda at all.

I went out the back door to find out how Mum was. She was still crying and surrounded by my sisters. I approached them all to ask Mum how she was and to ask her what was wrong.

I was about to have one of those moments. You know those moments that are etched deeply in your psyche. Moments that you will never ever forget. The ones that just seem to slow right down, so you don't miss a thing.

It was Leonie who turned to me, she was angry.

She said, *"What the hell is wrong with you? This is all your fault. Why don't you go back to who you were?"*

There it was.

"Why don't you go back to who you were?"

That was such a profound statement. It said so much in just a few words.

I was changing and I never considered how that impacted my family. The changes for me were liberating and exciting; I thought that would be the same for all those around me.

Rhonda had absolutely no right to try to hit me. But that wasn't how everyone else saw it.

This became my fault. That's how Mum, Dad and my sisters saw it. I wasn't having any of that. I demanded that my dad step up. This was his house and he had to take charge and hold anyone who behaved like Rhonda to account.

It was unacceptable that anyone, no matter how troubled or how many drinks, should think it's okay to behave like a thug in his house. What was he going to do about it?

I was asking him to change. I was asking him to step up and look out for me. I was asking him to start dealing with things.

He didn't do anything.

For some time, I kept at him, and he would say he would get back to me. I thought this was a very reasonable request. I wanted to be able to visit without concern for my safety.

In the end, he just couldn't do it.

Working on myself was taking deeper and deeper levels. I was 'feeling' myself and the world more. I was considering my thoughts and actions more. I wasn't feeling anxiety and worry all the time and my mind was getting clearer.

It had been a long time since I could actually feel tired and go to bed. Most times I had to make myself go to bed and then battle with my mind to stop thinking.

This was starting to change for the better.

I found myself one Saturday afternoon all alone.

The kids were with David, and I had the house to myself. I sat myself in front of my *IBM* typewriter.

OPEN HEART

I wanted to write a letter to my nan.

Nan and Pop had lived in Deniliquin, married and raised their kids there and, after 60 years of marriage, were finally selling up and moving on. They both were getting old and needed a little more support and attention, so they were moving to Melbourne, to my Auntie's place in Laverton to live.

They were putting their house on the market and, their home of 60 years needed to be sorted through and cleared out. My mum had met up with her two sisters a number of times to go through all the belongings.

I was concerned to hear that there were some arguments going on about who was getting what; you know that sort of stuff I'm talking out. It upset my mum and I'm pretty sure it was upsetting my nan as well.

So, that Saturday afternoon, I decided to write a letter to my nan and show her my support during such a difficult time. For a number of hours I wrote, I cried, I screwed up sheet after sheet of paper and began to write the letter time after time after time.

I got angry and sad, angry and sad at so many different people; it was cathartic. By the end of it all, I had the final letter and a huge sense of relief. What an afternoon.

My Return To Love

A hell of a transformation had just taken place for me, and I felt like such a weight had been lifted.

Next time I saw my mum, I gave her the letter. I asked her to give it to Nan the next time she saw her.

My Nan and Pop were pillars of the Deniliquin community and, as such, were visited by the local newspaper who wanted to do an interview and article about them both. My Nan was so touched by my letter she insisted that it was included, in full, in the newspaper article. It was accompanied by a photo of my Nan sitting outside their home and the quote read, *"Reading a heartfelt letter from her granddaughter Helen."*

Past Lives, Spirit Guides And Demons

■ Farewell...Leaving her home, Olive Henderson takes comfort from a letter written to her by her granddaughter.

After 88 years, Olive leaves Deni with happy memories

AFTER 88 years in Deniliquin Olive Jean Henderson has decided it is time to leave.

It is not a decision which has come easily to her, but she admits she simply can't cope living on her own anymore.

Mrs Henderson's daughter Elizabeth Cunningham is pleased to have her mum make the move to Laverton to live with her.

It will also put Mrs Henderson closer to her other daughters — Dorothy Taylor in Blackburn and Joy Watkins in Williamstown.

Mrs Henderson said it has been difficult to leave the town in which she has lived her entire life.

She was born Olive Jean Edwards, growing up on the property "Questa", opposite Twin Rivers on the Finley Rd.

She lived there until marrying Harold James Henderson, and the couple set up their own home in Lagoon St adjacent Deniliquin North Public School.

The Henderson and Edwards families have long associations with Deniliquin.

Mrs Henderson's mother was the first border at the local convent school, which she later attended herself.

Her father Robert was the Deniliquin alderman who gave his name to the RJ Edwards Reserve.

Mr Henderson was a well known teamster and his photograph hangs in the Peppin Heritage Centre.

Mrs Henderson said her husband was a retiring man, and even their wedding was conducted with a minimum of fuss.

They had been engaged for a couple of years and he was visiting her at Christmas when they decided on a trip to Melbourne to marry, "to avoid a big fuss about the whole thing".

To page four

Olive leaving, but with happy memories

From page one

The couple were active in the North Deniliquin Progress Association, the North Deniliquin Tennis Club, and helped organise the Back to Deniliquin celebrations in 1948.

With her daughters in Melbourne, Mrs Henderson has lived alone in her Lagoon St home since the death of her husband in September 1994. They had been married 63 years.

Although well supported by friends and family Mrs Henderson has decided it is time to leave.

The house which has been her home for the past 65 years has been sold. She is pleased the new owners have promised to take care of the garden she has so carefully tended and they have even invited her to visit whenever she returns to Deniliquin.

Last week family and friends held an afternoon tea to farewell her, with daughters Elizabeth and Dorothy on hand to pack and make the trip to Melbourne.

Mrs Henderson said it was hard to leave, especially when all her memories of Deniliquin were loving ones.

And to ease the heavy heart she takes out a letter written to her by her granddaughter Helen Taylor, to read and to share with all those she will miss, and as inspiration to others making changes in their lives.

She has requested this letter be published.

Dear Nan

I just felt like writing a few things to you and do hope that my thoughts might help you through the testing time you are going through now.

There are so many positive things happening around you right now that can appear so negative because of other people's negativity. In other words, those other people are having trouble coping, not necessarily you.

While you have this time back in your house, remember all of the wonderful things that happened there. They are *your* memories, Nan, and belong to you, not the house. Whether you have the house or not, you still have those memories.

Walk around your house and the gardens and cherish the memories that surface within you. Once again Nan they are your memories and no one can ever take them away.

Give some thought to all the treasures you have collected over the years. They are yours and you are allowed to do with them what you want. Just be happy within yourself that you have given them to whomever you wished and be at peace with that.

Please Nan, also take time to reflect on your own life. Look at all the wonderful things you have achieved, the children you have raised, the knowledge and skills you have passed on to them and the many other people. Also your marriage and partnership with Pop.

I feel sure Pop is watching over you at the moment and he is admiring the strength and courage you have.

I admire these qualities you have. It is times like you are going through now that test our faith in ourselves.

You will see others around you seeming 'not to care' or 'caring only for themselves'. These people can appear very hard or cruel. Let these people be whoever they are Nan, but also keep in mind who you are and what you are about.

Isn't it funny that all people need to do is talk about things but this seems to be the hardest thing for so many people, 'being open and honest'.

What I am saying in a nutshell Nan, is to be who you are, enjoy the memories you are having now, enjoy your time in Deniliquin with loved ones and friends and most of all, take care of yourself.

I look forward to seeing you Christmas Day.

With love, Helen.

CHRISTMAS MEAT TREATS!

- Mokangers traditional old style hams.
- Mokanger style smoked cooked chickens and smoked cooked trout.
- Lamb hams

Above meats made and cooked at Mokanger Butchery

– ALSO –

- Rolled roast of pork with mango & Hazelnut stuffing

MOKANGER BUTCHERY
253 Cressy St, Deniliquin (03) 5881 1976

Who knew? I opened my heart up that afternoon, in just one afternoon, and I was never the same again.

When your heart is shut down; so is your vocabulary. You know when I was preparing to marry David, I can remember clearly saying to him – my emotional extent is 'good/bad, happy/sad' so don't expect anything else from me. What an extraordinary statement to make. I was telling him so many things, wasn't I?

When your heart is open; you can express yourself in many ways. It was truly liberating to me. I remember how pleased I felt one day when my mum asked me to write some heartfelt words in a card she had.

She said, *"Can you do it please? You know how to write that sort of thing."*

I was so happy because she was right. I did know how to write those sorts of things.

It's one thing to know you have changed yourself.

It's another thing again when someone else recognises that you have changed. There was another time, a birthday party, and I overheard my father-in-law commenting to my mum on how much I had changed, how he noticed I was more at peace.

I really struggled to find words to explain how that made me feel. Such gratitude, such deep gratitude comes close.

Having said all that, there are some people who will never recognise the changes.

My Return To Love

There are some people who will always choose to see you the same way, the old way and will see all the things that are 'wrong' with you.

I think that says more about them than it does you.

Chapter 8

KARMA, LIFE AND DEATH

UNFINISHED BUSINESS

My life had become a tug of war.

Half of me was moving forward, learning new things. I went from being a student in Sylvanna's self-development classes; to running them alongside her. I went from being the massage/healing practitioner to her business partner.

The other half of me was struggling with my relationships with David, Andrew and Steve. David was playing mind games with me; Andrew and I had slipped back into old toxic patterns and Steve; well Steve wanted more from our relationship than I was prepared to give.

I didn't see how much he liked me and that was becoming a problem.

Extraordinary things were about to happen, and they began with my hypnotherapy session with Sylvanna.

Sylvanna was a qualified counsellor and spiritual healer and had just recently completed her studies and became a qualified hypnotherapist.

She had been watching my problems with Andrew and suggested I do a hypnotherapy session with her. I jumped at it. I really wanted to figure out how to either evolve our relationship or end it and, to be honest, I think I was actually a pretty good 'case study' for her.

I didn't think I would be a good hypnosis candidate. I figured I was too strong minded or too controlling to be hypnotised. It turned out that wasn't the case at all.

The session began and, immediately, I found myself to be in two places at once. It was a strange feeling.

I knew I was in the room with Sylvanna, but I was now also in another room. It was a dressing room, and it was filled with beautiful mahogany furniture. I was standing in front of a dresser, and I was opening up the drawers one at a time. The drawers were filled with the most beautiful and expensive garments. Stockings, petticoats, undergarments mostly and, in one drawer, I lifted the stockings and grabbed a pistol that was hidden underneath. It was a very small pistol with an ivory inlay in the handle.

The room was my dressing room, and it was part of a large building that was a dance hall, bar and brothel. I was in Texas, sometime in the 1800s. It was the era of cowboys. I was the star attraction at the dance hall and, as such, lived a very good life with all the best of things that money could buy.

I was in love with the owner of the establishment. We had a relationship that was going nowhere. He loved me because I brought him lots of money. He saw me as a possession, as something that he owned. I wanted his love.

It was never going to work out. He slept with many other women. It was a classic case of unrequited love.

It seemed I had reached a point of no return. I planned to meet with him somewhere out in the desert and, when he arrived, I shot him.

I killed him.

He was Andrew.

Sylvanna brought me back into the room. I was shocked.

Andrew and I had spent a past life together that had so many parallels to this current world, to this current time.

Back then, he owned a dance hall, which was also a brothel. Currently, he owned a brothel. Back then, we were in a relationship, but it had me as the 'star employee' and him as the owner. Now, I had worked for him at his brothel and was in a relationship with him.

Back then, I shot him and killed him. Currently, I had been following an urge to get a gun license. I had obtained the relevant papers and was filling them out to have them filed. Consciously, I had no idea why I wanted to get the gun license. I had just convinced myself that, because I was pretty good with the air rifle we had as a kid, I wanted to see if I was still a good shot.

This was a hell of a lot to take in. You just can't argue with real personal experience. My experience confirmed for me that past lives were real, and karma was real.

And to top it all off... Andrew came around that very night to visit me. He was so happy with a new tattoo that he was having done and just had to show it off. He rolled up his right pants leg to reveal the image. It was from knee to ankle down the outside of that leg. It was only an outline at this stage, but it was very obviously the figure of a beautiful girl in an adorned bodysuit, crouched down with a cowgirl hat on.

It was me, that past version of me, in one of the bodysuits I used to wear on stage.

I was speechless.

The past and the current timelines were converging. The past life was repeating itself.

I was in love with Andrew all over again and he saw me as nothing more than something he owned. That explained so much. I wanted him to be 'in' the relationship with me, to treat me like his girlfriend, to buy me flowers, to take me out to dinner, to sleep with me every night. He didn't want or do any of that.

It also explained the beginning of our relationship. Remember when I said there was an electricity between Andrew and I. We were like magnets that something was pulling us together with such a force, such energy, I couldn't explain it back then, but I understood it now.

This force is karma.

For a moment, I let myself think further.

If I wasn't conscious of what was going on, if I wasn't aware of the past and the karma – what would happen?

Would I have proceeded down the path of getting my gun license and then, would I have killed him?

I pondered further.

How many people were sitting in jail for crimes they committed based on karma? For crimes committed and they had no idea why they did it because some unconscious element was at play?

It was an incredible thought.

I have never really figured out what to call all these things that were happening to me.

The voices, the knowing, the coincidences, the learning. What was it all to be called? What was at work in my life? Was it God, the universe, divine consciousness or the great spirit?

Whatever it was, there was more in store for me.

WHAT ARE WE REALLY CAPABLE OF?

Only a few weeks went by before the next event. This was to be the culmination of my relationship with Steve. Unbeknownst to me; he had been projecting a great amount of energy and attention towards me.

It would seem he was trying to cast a spell or something to make me want to be with him romantically. This was all to be explained to me by Sylvanna, after the event.

It all began when I got sick. For a few days, I had been experiencing gastro type symptoms. I couldn't eat or drink and was losing a lot of energy. On this particular morning, I rang Sylvanna and told her I wouldn't be coming into work for the day. She explained that it would probably be best if I did come in.

She stressed that I didn't need to work but it would be better to have her to look out for me and keep me company. Essentially, she sensed something was wrong and would rather have me by her side than alone.

So, I did. I went around to her place and settled myself onto the couch. I could see her in the study nearby working and we could talk to each other if needed. I fell asleep; exhausted.

I woke sometime later and found that I had lost consciousness while asleep and had wet myself. I was so embarrassed and apologetic. Sylvanna reassured me and placed a kitchen chair in the middle of the room.

She got me up and made me sit on the chair. It was the strangest thing, but I was in no position to argue.

There was a reason behind what she was doing. She knew something wasn't right. This was much more than gastro. She kept repeating, *"Stay with me Helen, stay with me, stay awake, make sure you stay awake."*

She said she was going to gets towels and a flannel and would be back soon.

What happened next was astounding. I lost consciousness while sitting on that kitchen chair in the middle of the room. Then, I had a man standing to my right. He had a hold of my arm and was walking me forward. We came to another man, also to our right and he was standing behind a wooden podium. The podium had a large book open on it and he was flicking through the pages.

The man at the podium asked, *"What are you doing?"*

The man holding my arm replied, *"It's all okay, I'm just taking her through."*

They argued back and forward for a few minutes. The man at the podium was insistent; he didn't have my name down and he wasn't going to let us through. The man holding my arm also insisted that it was all okay and we should be let through.

Next, Sylvanna is slapping my face and saying, *"Helen, Helen, wake up, wake up!"*

I came to back into the room and was so disorientated. Sylvanna was happy to have me conscious again but she was also really concerned about something going on around me in the room.

My Return To Love

I was too weak and confused to do anything much at all.

Sylvanna encouraged me to have a shower and change into some fresh clothes and then we'd sit down to talk about what had just happened. I knew something significant had happened.

Gastro just wasn't enough to make you lose consciousness and it certainly didn't explain the weird experience I had with the two men.

She said she knew immediately from our phone call in the morning that there was something else going on. She knew she needed to have me by her side. She said, when I first lost consciousness, there was an extremely strong energy in the room with me and she was very concerned that I must not fall to sleep again.

That's why she put me on the kitchen chair in the middle of the room.

When she came back into the room, and I had lost consciousness again and she knew something awful was going on, she used all of her healing skills and abilities to break the connection and bring me back into the room.

She told me this had all been created by Steve and that she would speak to him about what had just happened. She didn't believe that his intentions were to harm me, but she doubted that he really knew the strength and potency of what he was actually creating.

She was right, Steve had no idea that he was harming me. He stopped whatever he was doing immediately and that was the end of any romantic notions between us.

We remained good friends.

BACK IN THE 'REAL' WORLD

We moved into another house. I had to because things with Andrew had gone from bad to worse again. I took out another intervention order. This time though the police officer said something important to me:

"What are you doing?"

This question certainly got my attention. He asked again, *"Why are you doing this? You're going to break this, aren't you?"*

Have you ever felt like you were talking to an angel? That's what that moment felt like.

I have no other way of explaining how profound his questioning was. It was like some greater power was talking straight at me, like he knew everything about me. His questions were the key to the way I would handle events up ahead. I just didn't know it yet.

But was the police officer right? He most certainly was.

The new house was free from crazy spirits and we all quickly settled in. We were instantly adopted by a beautiful British Blue cat. It seemed he had been left behind by some neighbours, so he become ours and we named him Shadow.

My self-development and energy work went to another level. Now I was seeing auras and spirits. Something in me had just switched on.

I have no other way of explaining it. I could physically see colours around people, and I could physically see or even sense spirits.

With the spirits, I could see smoky outlines, not the details. I could communicate with them in some strange way.

At the same time, my son Shane began to see things. He could see spirits in much more detail than me and even had a spirit guide called Rainbow Bird. It seemed that Rainbow Bird was around looking out for him.

What a crazy household we were.

I recall one time we were all sitting down to dinner. I felt a presence in the room, to my right, and I asked Shane, *"Who's here?"*

Shane said it was Pop and that he could see him standing next to me. We all said hello to Pop and got on with our dinner.

Steve was gone from my life now, a distant memory. He was another person, like Jane, who came into my life for a short period of time, a time full of incredible experiences and then was gone.

David was back in our lives, seeing the kids on a regular basis and had also begun to have some good conversations with me.

I welcomed these conversations. It was nice for the kids to see us getting along and I had always enjoyed David's insight into things.

More changes were coming my way. There is a reason why we can't see what's coming in life; because if we did, we would most certainly try to avoid it. I know I would have.

BREAKING THE SPELL OF KARMA?

Andrew was hovering around the edges of my life. Two intervention orders did not make the karma go away. I knew I had to find the answer and, I also knew, there was something I had to do to break the spell binding us together.

My feelings for him were still there and still very strong, but I was determined not to act on them in the physical world. I didn't want to break another intervention order. The police officer's words were still there in the back of my mind reminding me of something.

I just couldn't put my finger on it.

The spiritual path had various ways you could clear another person's energy, so I worked with various methods. Journaling, cutting the spiritual ties, mediation techniques, smudging… I tried many different ways to break the connection between us.

Andrew was in my dreams nearly every night, stalking me, haunting me and my anxiety and worry about the situation only grew. None of this stuff was working.

I surrendered. I threw everything up into the air and asked whatever higher power there was to help me.

What happened next was crazy.

Andrew had gotten my phone number again. Once again, David had passed it on. Just as before, David was the only contact between me and Andrew. Who else could it be?

Andrew started texting and calling. Here we went again…

I finally gave in and answered a call. He was a different person. He was kind, thoughtful and apologetic. He had come to the realisation of how badly he had behaved, how wrong he had been, and he wanted forgiveness. He wanted another chance and promised me I wouldn't regret it. He wanted to take me out for dinner.

You know he had never done that? Not once had we been out to dinner together.

Who was this man? He was everything I had asked for, everything that I had wanted. I was stunned but also hesitant. I had many questions.

How could he change so much?

That doesn't happen very often with people at all.

Could he remain this new version?

That was most important question.

I was full of doubt and told him I didn't want to see him. He kept ringing and I ignored the phone calls.

WHO WAS THIS NEW VERSION OF ANDREW?

He turned up at the front door.

"David," I thought to myself, *"How did Andrew know my address?"*

He wanted me back, he wanted me to talk to him, he had a ring. It was a sapphire and diamond ring, and he wanted me to have it as a gift.

I wouldn't accept it.

Accepting it meant I was about to accept so many other unspoken things. There was no way I was going to accept it and there was no way I was going to let him come into the house.

The whole thing escalated, he got angry, and I shut the door.

The phone calls continued.

I agreed to go out with him to dinner and it was horrible. We went to a pub and had a meal. It was embarrassing. I had only ever known one side of Andrew and that was the brothel business owner and drug dealer. In that world, he was confident and in charge.

At dinner, out in public, I saw another side of him. He was totally out of place, and it was uncomfortable for both of us. We had nothing much to talk about, so we ate and left.

I was changing and it was obvious to me that I had outgrown Andrew. I didn't want that world anymore. From Andrew's perspective, he had me back and that was all that mattered to him.

My Return To Love

At this same time, I needed a new car. The car I had was old and was going to cost more and more money to keep it going. This just didn't make sense, so I had decided I wanted a new car. It just so happened that Andrew knew someone who had a car that was exactly what I was looking for and at the right price. Andrew was still displaying this new version of himself, and he was keen to do whatever he could to make me happy.

The deal was made. I went and picked up the car and would have the money to Andrew within a few days.

It was a beautiful Saturday afternoon. Sylvanna was around visiting with me, and we were sitting in the lounge room with the French doors wide open enjoying the sunshine and a cup of tea. The kids were playing outside in the garden.

Something was making me feel uncomfortable. I went to check my phone. I had missed a few calls from Andrew, so I rang him. He immediately jumped down my throat and accused me of deliberately avoiding him.

He didn't hear me, he was yelling and screaming at me. He said he was at the *Croydon Hotel* and demanded I come and bring him the money immediately.

I told him I would deliver it as soon as my visitor had left, and I could find someone to look after the kids.

He went nuts over the phone. I hung up on him a few times, but he would ring back full of venom and extremely volatile. This was the drugs at work. I had seen it many times before where he would 'lose it' like this. I wasn't going to answer any more calls. I couldn't talk to him when he was like that.

The phone calls had put me on edge. Sylvanna tried to calm me down, but I was concerned about his behaviour and worried about what he might do.

As it turned out, my concern was warranted.

ANDREW THE PSYCHO

About 15 minutes later, I heard his car coming down the road. I knew the sound of it intimately. I heard it park outside the house and I was instantly on high alert. I went to close the French doors, but Andrew had already rushed around the side of the house and was on the other side of them. He was too strong for me and pushed the doors back open.

He was out of control and lunged straight at me, picked me up and started throwing me around.

I recall Sylvanna trying to talk to him and knew that the kids had scattered out of the room. I don't know how long this all took but next thing, the police arrived. They arrested him and took him away. He had broken an intervention order.

I had a few cuts and bruises but was mostly concerned about my kids and what they had just witnessed. Sylvanna was great. She had been the one to phone the police. She took care of me and boys until we had all calmed down.

I was now determined to find out how to break this invisible bond between Andrew and I. It was obvious to me that we were living in two very different worlds and that this would never work out. But how to break the bond?

It came to me one day from out of the blue.

It was a moment of inspiration. I had to do what was true to me, what I most wanted in my heart.

BREAK THE SPELL

It was ridiculously simple when I realised what I truly wanted but was also something that would be seen by most people to be the craziest thing to do.

Even my mind thought it was the craziest thing to do. That's why I had such a conflict going on inside me. My mind and heart were fighting each other.

The heart always won.

I loved him deeply, there was no denying that. What I now knew was I had to do what my heart wanted. I had been denying that. It wanted to be with him forever. I knew the answer now, I had to follow it to break the spell.

I called him and asked him to meet me at a park that I really liked. He arrived and I could see he was concerned about what I was going to say or do. I immediately put his mind at rest and told him I had done a lot of thinking.

I told him how much I loved him and that I would do anything to be with him for the rest of my life. Then, against what any of my friends or family would have agreed with, I asked him to marry me. I said I wanted me and the children to be with him, to live with him whether here in Victoria or South Australia, where he originally came from and that I would do whatever he wanted to make it work.

Boom, I could feel it.

I had broken the spell.

He was speechless for a while and, when he gathered his thoughts, said he would have to think about. He said my behaviour lately had made him question our relationship and what he wanted to do. I agreed with him. Of course, he could have time to think.

Then he got in his car, and he ran, he ran away from me so fast that the whole world was spinning. I knew, I knew that the spell was broken. All it took was for me to say what was deep in my heart and as soon as the heart spoke, it was over.

Love.

My love broke the spell.

Chapter 9

I 'KNEW' IT WAS TIME TO SWAP ROLES

I was back working with Sylvanna. A few months earlier, Sylvanna had approached me to talk about the business and us working together. She had come to the realisation that Andrew and I were not finished and was concerned because Andrew affected my behaviour, my energy and, ultimately, the business.

I was initially hurt and defensive about her comments but soon came to realise she was right. I had to leave her and the business and sort these things out for myself.

So, I was back working with her. We both agreed that my relationship with Andrew was over, and I was ready to walk this alternate path with her.

My Return To Love

There were a number of things going on for me. Raising my children was important. They were all boys and there was a lot of testosterone flowing. I was very aware of the changes taking place for them all and encouraged them to watch TV shows and read books I got from the library about their development.

At the same time, I was very aware that David was missing them. He made comments from time to time, and I certainly took note. Something was brewing in me. It was another one of those 'knowings'.

It was telling me to swap roles with David. To move out of the house and let him move in.

What an incredible thought. I had come to trust the knowings I had. I knew I would follow it, I just had to work out how. It provoked so many thoughts and emotions in me and I had to process them. Part of my processing was to talk to a few other people.

My mum was always a good one to talk to. She always listened; she didn't have the answer but letting me talk it out was valuable. Whenever I did this with her, I would always come away with more insight than I started with.

I only spoke to one other person and boy, was that a mistake. Jewell was a friend and had also been a client. She ran her own hairdressing business and was currently going out with a man named Steve. Jewell's lifelong dream was to marry Steve and have a family.

She was disgusted in me. She was horrified that I, the mother, would ever consider handing the full-time role of caring for the children to their father.

I 'Knew' It Was Time To Swap Roles

Told you, wrong person. We parted ways after that. It had become my mode of operating now. If someone judged me like that or directed their own anger, hate or blame at me, I removed them from my life. It was my internal mechanism that made sure I always had people surrounding me who were loving and supportive.

Next, I asked the kids what they wanted to do, who they would prefer to live with. This was such a stupid idea. I didn't know immediately but I learned that children will never choose a parent. It was awful thing to ask of them. It was up to me and David to work it out.

I really had to sit with this idea before speaking about it. I thought the idea through. I looked at it from every angle, the children, David and myself.

When I was ready, I spoke with David and he immediately jumped at the idea, but I told him to slow down a little, we had to plan how it would happen. We had to speak with the children and let them know what was happening first and then work from there. And we did.

We swapped roles. I moved out.

I took with me my personal belongings and my bed. That was all I needed really. I moved into a friend's house. I had a bedroom and access to kitchen and laundry etc. It wasn't easy, I missed my children. I didn't realise that I was giving up a huge part of myself, but I was willing to adjust. I had to. I really thought the change was the best for everyone.

It was time for another shift in my reality.

I was about to learn the meaning of impermanence and the importance of recognising when I had to sacrifice myself in order to help others to grow through their choices and experiences. It will all make sense, I promise.

I had surrendered my life and my children in order that we could all grow. I was now living a life with very little to my name. I was still working with Sylvanna, but I was starting to struggle. I wasn't consciously aware I was struggling but my behaviour said it all.

THROWING CAUTION TO THE WIND

I started drinking a lot of alcohol and spending my spare time with Steve (a new Steve) who also lived at the house. He was a musician and I just loved listening to him sing and play guitar. We spent many hours out on the balcony of the house drinking and enjoying each other's company.

His story – his marriage had fallen apart and he had split from his wife and given her custody of his son. Not long after separating, he struck up another relationship and had gotten engaged to this new woman. They had recently split, and he was a broken man.

We spent many hours talking about life and relationships. It became obvious to me that he just couldn't live without a woman, he needed one in his life for some reason. So, I became that next woman, but with me things were to be different. This wasn't to be a new relationship; this was a fling. We just filled a gap in each other's lives. Well, that's how I saw it. We were just having fun.

He kept texting and calling his ex-fiancé and then she would do the same. I watched this happening for a while and then confronted him. He was full of guilt and told me that they wanted to give it another go and had planned to spend a weekend together to see if they could make their relationship work.

He was absolutely blown away when I agreed. I encouraged him to do it and told him he had to find out once and for all if they could make it.

He couldn't believe that I was supporting to him, he thought I would get angry. I couldn't do that; I could clearly see that he needed to do it.

Ultimately, it didn't work. The weekend for Steve and his ex-fiancé was a disaster. Then I discovered his next problem, he thought that he and I were in a relationship. That wasn't the case and I made it clear to him. He unravelled and problem after problem began to turn up in his life.

Access problems with his son, a major car accident where he wrote off the car (he was okay), loss of music gigs which were his main source of income. He was falling apart.

Me, I was looking at moving to Queensland. An opportunity had arisen, and I was very keen to look at it. I made all the relevant plans and locked in a date to leave. The funny thing was Steve thought he was going to come with me. He started talking about travelling around playing music and told me he was headed for Queensland, as well.

I had made it clear from the start that we weren't in a relationship, but he chose not to listen to any of that. I sat him down and made it quite clear that I was going to Queensland alone. The day I moved out of the house; he sulked in the lounge room and made it clear he wasn't going to speak to me, look at me or say goodbye.

Emotional immaturity is ugly sometimes.

I moved temporarily to Mum and Dad's place waiting for the day I was to leave.

My plane was booked, and Sylvanna was to pick me up and take me to the airport.

Everything fell apart though. Sylvanna was delayed with car trouble, and I missed the flight. I took this all as a sign that maybe I was not supposed to go to Queensland.

The situation needed to be re-evaluated.

The truth was, I was going to miss my kids terribly and this ultimately was getting in the way of me leaving. I was actually very relieved and realised that I had by trying to make myself okay with going. This was one of my fundamental flaws.

Many times in life, I have put enormous pressure on myself to make something happen. I was grateful for the current awareness because I knew that you can't change anything until you become aware of it.

So, here I was, back living at Mum and Dad's place. It was surreal but it would do until I figured out my next step.

I hadn't considered that moving back there was actually an opportunity for some healing.

I 'Knew' It Was Time To Swap Roles

It was.

I began to have nightmares and even irrational fears during the day of someone stabbing me. I recalled that I used to have these thoughts and feelings when I was a child. They were the beginning of my irrational fear of being stabbed one day; my irrational thoughts when I would hold a sharp knife sometimes; my irrational thoughts of how weird it would feel to actually stab a knife into someone's flesh.

Where did all this come from?

Could it be Dad's thoughts or could it be something malevolent in the house?

I didn't know but I did know it was scary enough and only happened when I was in that house.

Then things went to another level. It began one day when Dad and I were alone in the house. He started following me around like he used to. He started calling me names and putting me down. I was perplexed.

Did he really think this behaviour would work on me now?

I wasn't a child anymore.

I turned to face him and challenge him. I pointed out the obvious fact that I wasn't a child anymore and he could just stop with his ridiculous behaviour. It stopped him in his tracks.

I told him to never treat me this way again and declared that I would move out as soon as I could arrange it.

Evidently, there was some healing to be done.

TRUE INSIGHT BEGINS

Can you see what was happening to me?

It all started with that one event, when the voice that told me to get out. From that day forward, I was catapulted from one scenario to another.

Most people would call them problems, so did I at first. There were many moments when I asked myself why this was all happening to me?

But slowly, I began to comprehend. I was overcoming many seemingly broken parts of myself one by one.

Situation after situation gave me the opportunity to embrace something broken, to then rise above it and subsequently, heal it.

I was leaving broken pieces of myself behind. I was transforming my experiences and memories; I was rewriting the stories of my life.

I had found myself in so many different situations, different experiences and along the way I learned some very important things:

- Don't judge myself and others.
- Something far greater than ourselves is always at play.
- Keep an open mind and allow room for insight to occur.

Life wasn't done with me yet.

More incredible experiences were yet to come, and I must tell them to you because I'm telling them from a different perspective now.

I 'Knew' It Was Time To Swap Roles

One important aspect had changed for me. I was now totally aware; I was totally conscious of what was going on and I was learning how to navigate life in this new state.

I had progressed from unconscious to conscious. I could see this when using my hindsight. I was starting to see the value in hindsight and how important it was. You don't see the little changes along the way in life; you see them when you look back and review what has happened to you.

From this new state of being, I could now see what was going on in others and, if guided to, I could help them as well to see other ways to manage or handle their current dilemma.

I loved this and deeply appreciated the ability. I automatically knew I had to handle it with care.

I had greater insight, into myself, into others and into the situations that presented themselves. The following stories dramatically outline how this worked for me.

Steve was still around. He learned I hadn't left for Queensland and began to call and text me again. It seemed he had gotten over being the rude, selfish child he was when I left. Remember that one?

I did really like Steve, but by now, I realised I had another even bigger problem. I was pregnant.

This was a dilemma. Steve and I were over – even though we still spoke and saw each other occasionally, I knew we were over.

I had a lot of serious contemplation to do. I began sessions with Sylvanna to work through the idea of having another child. It was a difficult time in my life and there was much to consider.

Among the many things I considered, the dominate problems were many. Steve was in a bad place. He was divorced, had a broken engagement, struggled to see his son and be his dad, struggled with finding work, struggled with money and just about everything else in his life.

Me; I wasn't much better. I was divorced, struggled with money, struggled to see my kids, lived back with my parents and couldn't see anything better in the future.

I scheduled an abortion. Sylvanna came with me. I had no idea I was going to have to walk through a number of protesters to get the front door. They didn't matter much. A much louder noise was going on mentally and emotionally inside me. I was terrified.

The staff checked me in, got me changed, processed me through the counsellor and into the operating room. I was given an anaesthetic, woke up and it was over.

The pain post procedure was terrible. Twice in the following week, I actually passed out from the pain. I told no one else about what had just happened; the past had taught me how judgemental people could be but I'm pretty sure Mum knew that something was up.

She was supportive, but never said a word. She was very beautiful like that.

But what is wrong with the world? Miscarriages and abortions are significant events in a woman's life, but they are not supported or discussed openly and, because no one speaks of them, you just don't know what to expect let alone what is normal for the experiences.

David and the children moved into another house. It was through a co-operative and meant cheaper rent and outgoings. It was very nice, and I began to visit them regularly. I was still living at Mum and Dad's and had regular access weekends with the kids, as well.

HISTORY REPEATS ITSELF

Then something crazy started to happen.

On my regular visits to David and the kids, Jeff was there a few times. Remember Jeff? When I first met David, it was Jeff that I started seeing first.

Well, it seemed as though Jeff was interested in seeing me again and David made a point of letting me know Jeff's thoughts. I was really taken aback. I had no interest in Jeff at all and found it strange that he even had these thoughts.

Next thing though, David hinted that maybe we should give it another try.

Again, I was taken aback. I had no feelings for David anymore either but somehow, I knew that it was important for him to reconnect with me. He had unfinished business and again, that 'knowing', said to follow this through.

I can't remember exactly what he said or how this happened, but it did. We started seeing each other casually and I even stayed over a few nights. It must have been pretty confusing for the kids, now I reflect on it.

In no time at all, that was over. David came to the conclusion that we really were over, and we went back to being separated again.

I had great concerns about the kids. David wasn't the best at running a house and looking after them. There were things I saw and things the kids said that worried me. He was doing the best he could but he still doing drugs and had questionable friends hanging around.

Many times, I spoke with him about sharing the role of looking after the kids. Each time he would listen, but it never went any further. He always had excuses or reasons.

I had a thought in the back of my mind. It said I should take him to court and get custody of the kids. That thought terrified me, so I pushed it way to the back of my mind.

I had to move on, but I had no focus with my own life and no idea where I was going. I really struggled with this, more than I even knew at the time. Most of the struggle was buried deep inside and it was covered with many fears. It had been a really long time since I had dreamed for just myself and I was actually terribly scared about that.

DEATH, AURAS AND CHURCH

I took up personal care work, firstly working with the physically and mentally disabled people. I studied and gained qualifications along the way and really enjoyed this entire new field of work.

I 'Knew' It Was Time To Swap Roles

I was good at it; I could read people and situations quickly, could adapt to different circumstances and was certainly someone you wanted around during a crisis – so I found out. I never knew that about myself.

I moved onto aged care. What a crazy environment to work in. I'm talking about the office politics, the management structure, the hierarchy of carers. It was a mine field of many personalities and behaviours – and that's just the staff I'm talking about.

Then, there are the residents. I learnt how to take care of them, look after them and, most importantly, respect them and the difficulties they faced.

Here's a snapshot of what I experienced.

My first dead body.

Sorry to sound a little harsh, but I need to get to the point. I hadn't considered this part of the job. It was totally unnerving the first time. To be present when somebody actually dies. Then I had to deal with the actual dead body; to wash, dress and present the body for the family viewing. It was scary, but also such a beautiful thing to have the honour of taking care of someone in that way.

I began to see auras again. This time is technicolour. I would walk into a resident's room that was filled with a green hue… Everywhere. I even walked into an estate agent office and experienced the same green hue all around the person at reception. This time around, I understood the colours more and embraced the situations as best I could.

I learned how to help the elderly as they struggled with the concepts of death, the ideas of heaven and hell and their daily struggles with having their lives upturned. It was incredibly rewarding but extremely hard work.

Then I had to move on. Disability and aged care had taught me about humility, respect and fostered a deeper compassion for the human spirit, but I just couldn't take the heavy load that came with all of that anymore.

I also couldn't handle these abilities I had, seeing auras, seeing spirits around the elderly as they were getting ready to pass over. I wanted it all to stop because I just didn't know what else to do with it.

I told myself that if seeing auras was a right brain, bigger picture capability then, maybe if I went back into law, which was predominately a left brain, detail driven realm, then maybe the auras would turn off.

So, I went back into law and started as a law clerk for a local suburban law firm. At this time, I had also moved into the hills. I really needed to get away from suburbia and into the country, the trees and fresh air.

The auras didn't stop.

There were two significant situations I recall. I walked into the boss's office, and he was sitting at his desk typing fervently on his computer. The ghost of a judge was behind him and leaning over him, watching what he was typing. I knew immediately that the boss was channelling information and insight from the judge.

I 'Knew' It Was Time To Swap Roles

It was incredible to watch.

The judge had the wig and velvet robe and was very regal looking. I said nothing.

The second event was when the boss came out to speak to myself and my work colleague.

He was very focused on what he was saying and, as he spoke, purple misty energy was flowing out and around his hands. I said nothing about that either, but I knew that this ability of mine was not going away anytime soon.

I enjoyed my new work colleague. She was a younger, very religious woman. We had many good conversations about faith and God which really struck a chord with me. I loved that she had such a trust in something other than herself and she had built a strong foundation within herself. I really admired that and also realised that I didn't have anything like that myself.

What did I rely upon when things got difficult?

I realised I had nothing to rely upon. I wanted to change that. I wanted to find out how to have a strong inner faith that I could lean upon when times were tough.

So, I decided to revisit the whole concept of church. My experiences as a child were of being made to go to church and I had resented that because church just seemed so silly to me.

Even though I was a child, I knew that something wasn't quite right about church, the concept of sin, the bible stories, going to confession, so now, as an adult, I revisited those thoughts and experiences.

I went to a local service and just loved the energy of the whole room. It was filled with community and an enormous amount of love, but it was the words that the minister spoke that concerned me. The things he said just didn't ring true to me, so I decided to enrol in the Bible study class to look at things a little further.

In my first Bible study class, the minister spoke about the 'resurrection'. I was taken aback because, when he spoke, he had the image of a priest standing behind him. The priest was dressed in a white and red robe and had a large headpiece on, like a Cardinal has. He was channelling this priest.

I looked around the room hoping someone else could see what I was seeing. No, everyone was focused on his words. The minister finished speaking and I raised my hand. I asked if Jesus was a multi-dimensional being. I was trying to figure out how he could be dead, disappear and then reappear.

The minister wasn't very kind. He barked at me, *"We don't know, it's a mystery."*

I realised straight away that he didn't like my question. How could he just be happy with not knowing? I just didn't understand.

When the class was finished, everyone stayed around for tea and coffee. Many others came up to me and asked me about my question. I told them I was just trying to figure out what this whole Bible thing was all about. I didn't know if there were other dimensions, but it now seemed that the church also didn't know much more than that either.

We all had questions and, if the church didn't have the answers, I had to move on and find the answers elsewhere.

DID I JUST ASK TO LOSE MY LICENCE?

It was at this time that I was really starting to struggle again. I missed the children terribly and was drinking more alcohol than I needed to.

I didn't realise at the time, but I was using alcohol to push down the pain, to push down a myriad of emotions that were just too painful for me to face. I was so lonely and messed up inside. I knew I had a problem, but I just immediately justified it like this… I don't drink all the time, I could go days without drinking and then sometimes, I would drink way too much.

It wasn't about any of that; I just couldn't stop and that was the problem.

So, I said this out loud, *"Someone stop me, I need to be stopped. I can't go on like this anymore."*

On a Saturday afternoon, I had been talking on the phone to Sylvanna. We were still friends after all this time, and she had moved to the country to live. We had been on the phone for over two hours, and I had been drinking red wine. I had had four glasses of wine, 1/2 wine and 1/2 soda water – it was a clever way of telling myself I wasn't drinking too much.

My Return To Love

Now do you see the silly mind games I would play with myself?

I had run out of cigarettes and told her I would call her back after I drove up to the local supermarket to get some more.

I wasn't even sure if the supermarket would still be open, but I jumped into my car, drove to the top of my street, turned right onto the main road and right into a booze bus.

Be careful what you ask for. You just never know what form it will come in.

I lost my licence for 10 months.

I had to take a bus and two trains to and from work which added three hours per day in travel. I didn't get upset because I knew I had asked for this. I took everything in my stride – even the drink driving classes I had to attend and even the humiliation at having to admit what I had done to my friends and family.

Then my dad died. One minute he was in hospital, then things were going downhill, and they were going to transfer him, and next, we were all just standing vigil while he was unconscious and declining.

My experiences in aged care were now invaluable. I took some essential oils into the hospital with me, got a flannel and some warm water and proceeded to wash Dad's face, his neck and shoulders and his arm. My mum was a little taken aback but I reassured her it was okay to do this. It was a really nice thing to be able to do.

I left her with him and went outside to have a cigarette. When I returned, she was there with the flannel and gently washing

I 'Knew' It Was Time To Swap Roles

his arm. I was so pleased. It's so important to be able to connect with a loved one during the crucial time of dying.

He died early the next morning, and my brother and I said our goodbyes and left his room for the elevator.

What happened next was extraordinary.

Mark and I stood at the elevator waiting for it to arrive. Immediately, I felt a strong presence standing between us. I looked over to Mark and he was looking at me. I said, *"Can you feel that, too?"*

"Yes," he said softly.

I asked, *"Do you know who it is?"* and he replied, *"Yes, it's Dad."*

He was absolutely right. We were both aware that the energy of Dad was standing between us; it was such an incredible moment and we were both in awe of what had just occurred.

We got into the lift and made our way back to Mum and Dad's home and it happened again. We were sitting across from each other at the dining table when I noticed Dad standing to the side of Mark.

Immediately, Mark looked at me and said, *"He's standing next to me, isn't he?"*

I confirmed he was right; Dad was certainly standing there.

I have no idea why that had to happen but it was another one of life's moments that I was always remember. What an incredible experience for us both and, in some way, it opened up something for Mark because he went on to have many other unusual experiences over the next few years.

Life settled back into its rhythms, and I navigated seeing the kids on alternate weekends, doing the public transport thing back and forward to work – while trying to figure out where my life was heading.

Chapter 10

WILL THIS RIDE EVER STOP?

Life certainly wasn't finished with me.

My concerns about David's lifestyle and parenting skills started to mount. The 'knowing' within me got louder and louder. I had to take the children back.

I knew what I had to do; it was the last thing I wanted to do but I did it. I filed for custody.

I moved into Mum's home. I needed flexibility because, if I won, I would have to find a place close to their school.

Life dealt its hand.

Cameron found a syringe on the kitchen floor. He rang to tell me, and I told him to secure it and put it into his backpack and bring it with him to access that weekend. He was such a brave boy and, looking back, he should never have been put into that position.

He had grown so much while living with his dad. I could see that he was taking on the role of parenting his brothers and looking out for them. It was never ever meant to be his job.

As soon as they arrived for access, I rang David and let him know that the kids were not coming back to him. I got custody and we all moved into a new home together. David indirectly confirmed that he had been waiting for me to do something. He was just never going to admit it.

It was difficult at first. The kids were not used to boundaries and rules anymore and I had to set about changing all that. And I did change all that. I saw that my job as a parent was to provide a good, safe environment for them to grow and to teach them how to navigate life by learning and taking responsibility along the way.

There was some kicking and screaming along the way, but we all made it through.

EVOLUTION WAITS FOR NO ONE

I continued to evolve and learn during this time and stumbled upon a healing modality based in Ecuador called Adamantine System. I trained personally with the developer Dr Francisco Rosero and had extraordinary results.

I stopped smoking overnight.

All thoughts associated with smoking were totally gone from my mind. It was incredible but there were repercussions to come. You see, smoking actually suppresses emotions and when I stopped smoking, those emotions were released, and I began to experience problems with my nervous system. This developed into problems with my lungs and on it went.

I got sick; very, very sick.

I went to the doctor. I had x-rays and scans and was given the prognosis.

I had cancer.

There was no way I was going to follow the medical model. I knew I was going to manage this myself and with the help of alternative therapists and products.

It was a daunting prospect, but I did it. I put one foot in front of the other and slowly addressed every aspect of my life. It's not easy to do that when you are feeling overwhelmed and exhausted.

I had the support of two alternative practitioners that I also called my friends, and I will be forever grateful to them for their help. They knew, as I did, that I was on the path to death and that was a tremendous reason to get better.

I was in no position to care too much about myself at that time. I was struggling but, once again found, that when you struggle to do something for yourself it can be easier to find another purpose. Once again, my children were the reason for me putting one foot in front of the other. I'm not sure where I would have been without them.

As my health improved, so did my outlook. I found a new job and we also moved into a new home. This was a bigger home because, this time, we had my sister and nephew come to live with us, as well. It was wonderful time.

I began meditation classes from home and started seeing clients for various treatments that I offered.

FROM MEDITATION TO TELEPATHY

Then another ability decided to emerge. It wasn't auras. This time, it was telepathy.

I worked in an environment with many people spread out over one entire floor and all sitting at pods. I think it was about four people to each pod. I was in image processing and there were call centre staff, as well. It was open plan and always busy and buzzing along.

I was in the middle of my shift, when a voice out of nowhere said, *"Tell him to tell her I'm okay."*

This wasn't like the 'get out' voice. This one was coming from inside my head, but I knew it wasn't me.

She was clear and she was insistent, and I knew who she wanted me to speak to because I was looking directly at him when she spoke. She was talking about my manager. His name was Frank.

Will This Ride Ever Stop?

There was absolutely no way I was going to tell Frank that some voice in my head had a message for him. She wouldn't stop though. All through my shift she kept up.

She was there the next day and the next day. I didn't know what to do.

Out of desperation, I made a deal with her. I told her that if I happened to have the opportunity to speak directly with Frank, I would tell him.

Well, guess what happened?

The next day, I was late for work and struggled to find a car park, so I parked in a spot reserved for management and vowed to move my car during my break.

During my break, I went downstairs to move my car. There was a note on the windscreen, a terse note, telling me never to park there again. It was from Frank. I had actually parked in his spot. Can you believe it?

I raced back into work to continue my shift. 10 minutes in, along comes Frank and he makes his way straight over to me. He isn't happy and makes a point of telling me off about the parking. I tell him it won't happen again.

And then, BAM.

The voice was back and very insistent that I speak with him now. I promised, didn't I?

I found some courage and blurted it out. I told him I have a voice speaking to me and she wants me to give him a message. He went white and I was concerned he was going to pass out.

We went somewhere quiet to talk further. It turned out the voice was the mother of his wife. She had died in a car accident when his wife was a little girl and she had always blamed herself for causing the accident and killing her mother.

So, so tragic.

Once he got over the initial shock, he was incredibly pleased that he had a message to relay to his wife and with the hope that she could maybe put this to rest because it had haunted her for most of her life.

This was incredible but it didn't stop there. We had massive bushfires take place not long after that and a number of people died. Many people at work knew some of the families and loved ones and, on two separate occasions, emotional conversations were taking place next to me.

On both of these occasions, spirits would come through to me with messages and I would pass them onto my work colleagues. The messages brought comfort and were never questioned.

I saw in my mind's eye a long, long line of people waiting to speak through me. It was overwhelming, so I shut the internal door.

I was not willing to be a conduit for the deceased.

Will This Ride Ever Stop?

I did hear, however, that word was going around the office floor that I was a witch. I laughed to myself.

I knew the source of the rumours but was still stunned that here, in the 21st century, there were still fearful narrow-minded people.

It was nothing new to me. I've lived most of my life on the edge.

Chapter 11

REVELATIONS

At first, I saw my whole journey as a spiritual one. Exploring crystals, tarot, healing, discovering myself and then moving into opening my heart, forgiving others.... You probably did, too.

But it's actually a journey back home, back to who I really am. Maybe it's even the hero's journey that seems to be woven into so many storylines in movies and books.

I know it was a journey designed for me to reclaim myself and to realise some very important truths along the way. It was a journey designed to call me back within myself and to reconnect with a higher source, a higher power, something I have always simply called 'love'.

I have learned some truths through all my life experiences. When you experience things, you know things, you don't just believe.

My experiences encouraged me to dig deeper and find out why we are wired the way we are, why we think the way we do, why we behave the way we do. I had to learn about it all. I was no longer going to just 'believe' what I was being told.

I learned that, from the time we are born, we are encouraged to focus on everything 'outside' of ourselves. That activates and strengthens our belief in the mind and our reliance on our five senses. The mind and senses are completely plugged into the external world. These can also be known as our lower operating modes.

We ultimately surrender our consciousness, our soul and intuition, our magical, internal world, and learn to totally focus on the external world. Even as a little girl, I knew this was wrong and, through many questions, I learnt that none of the adults around me had the answers.

I learned that when we function completely using the 'mind' and our five senses; the natural 'inner' workings begin to diminish. Our innate trust in ourselves, in God, in life and our ability to flow with life, literally die.

Remember there were many times I was conscious that there was something else walking along the path of life with me. So, what was that? My higher self, spirit guides, God?

There were so many unanswered questions.

How did I immediately stop drugs overnight, stop smoking overnight?

What was it that spoke out loud to me?

Revelations

What was it that thwarted my attempt at suicide, that made Andrew drop me when I was about to die?

What helped me open my heart in an afternoon?

What guided me to surrender to a nervous breakdown that took only one night and shifted me into a completely different, more positive outlook on my life?

And what about the new abilities I found along the way?

How was I seeing auras and spirits and the deceased? How was I able to hear people that weren't a direct part of this reality?

I was able to see beyond my physical eyes and to hear beyond my physical ears. I was to learn that these are higher functions available to everyone not just me.

When we stop relying on and using only our five senses, we tap back into higher senses.

And then the most important higher function of all – the 'knowing'. It's an internal guidance system that always directs us along the right path. The knowing inside me strengthened along the way. I no longer question it and it never leads me astray.

I can now see that, as I challenged and exposed each story/event/program that I encountered, I overcame them. I was actually breaking old cycles and old patterns. Some were mine; some were my father's; some were my mother's.

The cycles just couldn't continue anymore.

So, is there some truth in the hero's journey I spoke of earlier?

Maybe the hero's journey is a signpost; a metaphor that is hinting at what we must do.

We must walk a path in this life, and it must be our own path; not the path of someone else or of the tribe. We must walk it consciously and we must navigate certain obstacles along the way. As I navigated and overcame those obstacles, they had no power over me anymore and seemed to turn into mist.

Are those obstacles creations of the mind?

When we operate from the mind and our five senses and when we believe that everything happens outside of us; does that limit us?

You bet it does.

After years of living via the senses of the outside world, the voice called me back within myself, calling me back to God, my soul, whatever that is, I still struggle to give it a label, and events along the way encouraged me to listen only to my 'knowing' and to trust the quiet voice within me.

All my experiences in this book were limitations of the mind.

No sooner had I conquered one, I walked straight into another one. Event after event after event – until I finally broke free.

I don't regret the spiritual journey.

Each of those experiences helped me open my heart and reconnect strongly with my inner knowing and intuition. Each experience

Revelations

helped me question and study 'the mind', my senses and every other thing that I had been taught along the way.

I have always questioned everything but the experiences I have shared with you taught me to also research and investigate everything I had been taught because we have not been taught or shown the truth about this world at all.

I am talking about the truth of who we are; the truth about how the world works; the truth about everything.

The actual process of writing this story revealed the deepest and darkest parts of myself. I hope it also shed some light for you because that was my goal.

I will never stop learning and sharing.

I will never stop freeing others from the fear and limitations of their own minds.

If I can do it; then so can you.

You are the greatest creation on this Earth.

Start acting like it.

AFTERWORD

I've known all along that I'm not from here. I spent much of my life trying to fit in, to mold myself to the expectations, programs, and projections of others, but it never felt right.

It took time for me to realize that we're not here to fit in—we're here to be ourselves, to live a good life in the most authentic way possible.

For so long, I got caught up in other people's programs—society's programs, cultural norms, and expectations—until I became versions of myself that weren't true to who I was. I was lost.

It happens to us all. We live in illusions, disconnected from our true nature.

The path of spirituality pulled me into places that were dark and heavy, filled with demons, ghosts, and negative energies. It was part of my learning, but it was not my truth.

My Return To Love

True power comes from knowing who you are at your core, understanding how you really operate, and recognizing what you are truly capable of.

The turning point came with Adamantine Healing—it opened the door and showed me the way back to myself.

Through a simple practice of meditation and healing I began to guide my life. The journey I embarked on taught me how to operate correctly in this realm and start living my best life.

We enter this world surrounded by mental energy, and from the moment we're born, the game begins. That's why I wrote this book.

I want people to understand the nature of this mental energy, the programs, the projections, the egregores that dominate our experience. People need to know how this realm really works—how the mind traps us in patterns that separate us from our true source.

Adamantine Healing helped me break free. It taught me how to take control of my mind, care for my body, and deepen my connection with source.

It showed me the combined power of the present moment and the magnetic heart, where true internal manifestation begins. The more aligned we are, the more opportunities appear—this is what it means to truly create from within.

At a cellular level, this is where science and experience meet. While some look to scientific proof, for me, the experience is the proof.

Afterword

Equanimity, maturity, balance—these are the results of this healing journey. Francisco brings in the science to support it, while I've always found that the experience itself is what validates the truth.

People all over the world are waking up to the truth. They are realizing they are not their minds or bodies, and that realization is liberating. It's wonderful to witness.

My mission is clear: I am here to help others return to their natural state—free from the confines of the mind, deeply connected to source, and living with clarity, balance, and purpose. This, to me, is heaven on earth.

Through Adamantine Healing, we can do anything. It's why I reconnected with Francisco.

He has a step-by-step system designed specifically to show others who they are and what they are capable of and now it's available in Australia.

People everywhere are waking up to their power, and I am here to help guide that journey.

This book is not just my story—it's an invitation for you to explore your own truth and your own power. We are all capable of creating a new reality, and I am honored to walk this path alongside you.

With love and gratitude,
Helen

ABOUT THE AUTHOR

Helen has many labels. She is a daughter, sister, mother, friend and teacher. She has been a law clerk, conveyancer, healer, massage therapist, counsellor, life coach, ordained minister, doctor of metaphysics, chiropractor and a public speaker.

Her life's path has been a solitary journey; a passage through the most profound depths of existence. It was as if the universe deliberately placed her through the wringer, subjecting her to trials and tribulations that could only serve to elevate her into a role of profound service to humanity.

At the core of life's darkest moments, she discovered what she was being asked to do. She was being asked to help eliminate the suffocating fear that shrouds us all. Not just any old fear but the very fear of ourselves, the most primal fear of all. It was the common theme through every one of her experiences and it became her greatest gift to share.

Helen understands that her journey through solitude was not in vain. It was the very thing that forged in her the strength, empathy and wisdom needed to be a catalyst for her own change.

With every step, Helen is committed to lifting the veil, helping others to realise that they too can move beyond the illusion, beyond fear, and step into a world of unity, empowerment and limitless possibilities.

ADAMANTINE HEALING AUSTRALIA

If you're ready to explore a path of true self-discovery, healing, and alignment with your inner source, I invite you to join the Adamantine journey.

This transformative practice is now available in Australia, empowering individuals to take control of their minds, hearts, and lives. Visit Helen's website to learn more about how Adamantine Healing can help you live a balanced, purpose-driven life and discover the steps to creating your own reality.

Take the first step toward your true potential—join us on the Adamantine journey and find your way to a life of clarity, equanimity, and fulfillment.

Website : www.helentaylor.com.au
Email : helen@helentaylor.com.au
Mobile : +61 405 751 098

NOTES

www.ingramcontent.com/pod-product-compliance
Lightning Source LLC
Chambersburg PA
CBHW041316110526
44591CB00021B/2809